...and so together they traveled over the rainbow bridge
and down the spiral staircase until they came to a big gate.
The child felt a little anxious about leaving his wonderful home,
but with courage in his heart and his Angel beside him,
he went through the gate and
a little baby boy was born upon the earth.

Awards for
Beyond the Rainbow Bridge:
Nurturing our children from birth to seven

Independent Publisher Book Awards
2001 Finalist — Parenting category

iParenting Media Awards
2003 Winner — Best Products

Beyond the Rainbow Bridge

Nurturing our children from birth to seven

BARBARA J. PATTERSON AND PAMELA BRADLEY

Edited by Nancy Parsons

Illustrated by Jean Riordan

Beyond the Rainbow Bridge:
Nurturing our children from birth to seven

Published by Michaelmas Press

Michaelmas Press, PO Box 702, Amesbury, MA 01913-0016 USA
Phone: 978-388-7066, Fax: 978-388-6031 Email: info@michaelmaspress.com
Web site: www.michaelmaspress.com

Publisher's Cataloging-in-Publication
(Provided by Quality Books, Inc.)
Patterson, Barbara J.
Beyond the rainbow bridge : nurturing our children from birth to seven / by Barbara J. Patterson and Pamela Bradley. — 1st. ed.
p. cm.
Includes bibliographical references.
LCCN: 99-67459
ISBN: 0-9647832-3-1
1. Child rearing. 2. Child development. 3. Early childhood education. 4. Parenting. I. Bradley, Pamela. II. Title.
HQ769.P38 2000 649'.12
QB199-1452

10 9 8 7 6 5

Printed in the United States of America

Footnoted references used with permission of the publisher Anthroposophic Press/SteinerBooks (Great Barrington, MA).

To all children everywhere
especially those who have been
our greatest teachers

Table of Contents

Foreword

Parents today are flooded with a myriad of choices in raising children, complete with scientific studies to support each alternative. We need time, courage, and patience to thoughtfully consider each of these choices, especially in our children's formative years — the first seven years of life.

Barbara Patterson, a seasoned Waldorf teacher, clearly states: "What may seem 'normal' or acceptable in society today is not necessarily what is 'healthy' for families and children."

Barbara presents a perspective of child development based on the work of Rudolf Steiner, the founder of Waldorf education. Steiner's picture of children's readiness and needs at each stage of development can supply guidance for parents and teachers to establish a healthy foundation for life.

So significant is this approach to learning that in the more than 80 years since the first Waldorf/Steiner school opened, this independent educational movement has spread globally resulting in more than 700 schools in 46 countries.

In her common sense way, Barbara weaves Steiner's insights with the comforting, wise advice of a master teacher and grandmother who has a deep love and understanding of children and their needs.

Barbara's presentation of the material is clear, straight-forward and very accessible to parents. At the end of each chapter, participants in her parent-enrichment class voice real-life questions arising from the thoughts she has presented. Their questions and her responses place this book into a contemporary perspective.

For readers who may want to explore further, there are birthday stories, handwork instructions, a list of age-appropriate fairy tales, recommended reading, and Waldorf/Anthroposophical resources.

Beyond the Rainbow Bridge is a perfect book for new parents, grand-parents, daycare providers — everyone interested in the quality care of infants and young children.

Teachers, counselors, and health educators working with parent/infant or parent/toddler classes certainly will find this book a significant resource as well.

I am filled with gratitude to Barbara and Pamela for making this publication available.

— Janet Kellman
Director of Early Childhood Education
Rudolf Steiner College, Fair Oaks, California

Introduction

For many years I hoped to put together an introduction to Waldorf education. I would have welcomed such a book when my older daughter started in a Waldorf school some years back—a small book, readable, kept on the night stand to explore in a small dose each night. It would have given my husband and me a jump start on what was going on in our daughter's school, what the teachers were trying to accomplish, and what we as parents could do to make their jobs (and ours) a little smoother. But I didn't know how to get all that information into a small book, and I certainly didn't have all the answers about Waldorf education.

A light went on one day during autumn of 1995 as I read about an upcoming lecture series for parents to be given in the home of my daughter's beloved Waldorf kindergarten teacher, Barbara Patterson. This was the opportunity I had been waiting for. I had a feeling that Barbara knew what to say to parents, and that I would be able to fit her wise words into a small book.

On four consecutive Thursday mornings I joined Barbara's enrichment classes. Parents flooded in the front door of her home, quickly removed their children's coats and boots, and ushered their sons and daughters to childcare on the lower level of the house. Parents new and experienced, younger and older, from city and suburbs all joined together, filling the seats in the living and dining rooms. We were drawn together by a common denominator: our young children.

The participants agreed that these morning lectures should be shared. I'm delighted to have helped Barbara create this book — our gift to the Great Oaks School, a developing Waldorf school in the suburbs north of Chicago where she teaches.

Waldorf education continues to be a beacon for my family. It promotes healthy child development in a time often negligent of and even hazardous to children. I am very grateful to the Waldorf schools for nurturing the spiritual and physical health of my own children, and to Barbara Patterson.

Barbara is a true professional with uncanny instincts about the children in her care. Her love of children and her willingness to speak on their behalf is inspiring. A co-worker once said, "Mrs. Patterson's well-formed classroom rhythms are beautiful to see. She is always calm and present to the needs of the moment. I always felt that the rhythm created in her classroom was as soothing to me as an adult as it was for the children. She is a delight to work with, a wise teacher, and a model of how well Waldorf Education can work."

As you will soon see, it is impossible to separate Barbara's insights from her personal history because it is through her own unfolding life story that she has come to understand children so well. Her biography is a lesson in itself and the backbone to all that follows. Her message is as comforting to the adult in our fast-paced world as a fairy tale is to a child. Welcome to our wonderful meetings with Barbara Patterson!

— Pamela Bradley, Chicago, 1999

Editor's note on gender references:

I used plural, non-gender specific references where possible and effective. When I felt that speaking of a particular child was more appropriate, i.e., made the text more personal and immediate, I alternated the gender of the pronouns. So long as the text referred to the same child, the same gender was retained.

My Life, My Work, Our Children

A few years ago I wrote my mother a note of thanks. I told her how the rhythms and good habits she created around me during my childhood had influenced my adult life and my work with children. Mother was a homemaker *extraordinaire* in my youth, turning her everyday tasks into works of art. Even her laundry line looked like a painting: all the socks on the line matched, then came all the men's shirts hanging neatly side-by-side, then all the colorful kitchen towels flapping in the breeze.

My Parents' Home

As a child, I knew that Monday was wash day. I knew the beds would be changed and all the towels would be removed from the bathroom and replaced by fresh ones. I knew Tuesday was ironing day. I can still see all those shirts my mother ironed. She folded them and laid them on the dining room table in such a way that the second shirt came up to the collar point of the first, then the third to the collar point of the second, and so on, in one long line. She usually ironed twenty-one shirts a week! Similarly, the napkins and even the kitchen towels were ironed and ordered on the table. All this care in her work, which could have been painted by an artist, still lives with me and in my work.

I appreciate, especially now, what a gift she gave me. I did not have to learn to bring rhythm and good habits to my own children's lives and to the children of my classrooms. I already had them, inside. I had grown up with them.

Another important part of my childhood was doll play. At one point my mother wondered if I'd ever stop playing with dolls! But of course, she was the one who had cultivated this play form, sewing my clothes along with matching outfits for my dolls. My doll play evolved as my own stage of development evolved. In my early years, I was their pretend mother. In the middle years, I taught my dolls, setting them up in my own classroom. I would hang around at the end of the school year to see if my own teachers were discarding any books or papers I might use in my school.

As I got older I learned to sew for my dolls. I recently came across a pair of doll pajamas my mother had made. At some point in my childhood, a fastener came off at the neck of the pajama top. I hacked a crude hole into the fabric and sewed a button to the opposite side. When my mother saw this, she said I needed to sew around that button hole so it wouldn't unravel. I can still see, some 50 years later, those original stitches I carefully sewed around the hole I had so crudely made.

These early experiences led me into my career as a teacher of young children. Not only do my classroom dolls still wear some of the clothes my mother made, but the children enjoy doll play as much as I did.

The doll corner was always a strong focus in my classroom, even among children who didn't otherwise play with dolls. Over the years, parents and teachers have asked me how I engaged children in this type of play. It came naturally to the children in my classes because of my own love of dolls.

In the same way that my mother and I bonded over dolls, my father and I bonded in the evenings over some corrective work I needed for a lazy eye condition. My father worked every night with me for an hour with a hand-held machine that was supposed to improve my eye coordination. He had already worked all day at his job and his work with me cut into the time he could have spent with my mother and brothers. He did this work with me for years, and I feel that the warmth of his love and dedication combined with the effects of these daily eye exercises continues to bring me strength for my life and for my work with children. Ironically, my father lost his own eyesight in later years, and he loved to have me read to him when I came for a visit.

He provided a stable home life for the family and was a very involved parent. I remember skipping along beside him on our Saturday morning shopping trips. People in the stores would comment that there was no denying I was his daughter. I looked just like him. Those were special times.

Meal times were also special. During supper, we loved to hear him tell stories of his youth or of when he was at college, and these stories made for happy family togetherness. My parents had been married for 65 years before my father died in 1995. The two of them truly gave me the gift of a solid and happy childhood with good role models to imitate. Their gift has strengthened me as a teacher.

My Home

My own children also taught me a lot about being a teacher. I learned again about consistency and rhythm from my own daughter. She was imaginative, social, and very lively. I discovered that confrontational discipline didn't work very well with her. Creating consistency and strong rhythms in our home was a more effective discipline tool.

My son was very different from my daughter. He was the more inward child, pale and thin with an early intellectual development. He was small for his age. From him I learned how important it is to protect a child's senses. He was so sensitive that he could run a fever after a trip to a crowded department store. Because of his early intellectual development, he could verbalize what he felt about my parenting methods, thereby educating his mother about things other children might only feel as an inner confusion.

He transferred to the Rudolf Steiner School[1] in New York City in the fourth grade, and the resulting changes in him were remarkable. At first, after watching his classmates playing a

[1] The oldest Waldorf school in North America, established in 1928.

beanbag game intended to reinforce the multiplication tables, he expressed concern that he wasn't going to get very smart in a school where they just played. But over time his intellectual side balanced with all the artistic activities at the Waldorf school, and he even grew physically. My parents, who knew nothing about Waldorf education, at one point said that they wouldn't have recognized him if they had passed him on the street. And he was able to put his intellectual skills to good use. Today he is a medical doctor.

I must say that I did not seek out Waldorf education for my children, but rather found it through my husband's work as a minister. I actually resisted Anthroposophy[2] in the beginning, not finding the inner connection between what Rudolf Steiner wrote and my own background of life experiences. But I tried to remain open to something my husband found very meaningful, and gradually came to value Steiner's teachings. I was most impressed with how quickly our children took up Waldorf education after five and three years in public school, respectively. My daughter's Waldorf teacher said that after about three days in the school, it was as if she had been there all along.

I became active in the school and went to parent evenings and classes in woodworking and even eurythmy, a movement art

---

2 Rudolf Steiner (1861-1925) was an Austrian-born philosopher who founded a spiritual and cultural movement called Anthroposophy — "knowledge of the true nature of the human being." See Appendix.

form created by Steiner. Before long, I knew I wanted to be a teacher, but I didn't know how I was going to get the necessary training. I continued to learn what I could about Waldorf education while raising my children.

I was a stay-at-home mom. Through our church I became involved with various children's programs, as well as summer camp and a teen youth group. We even had children boarding at our house. Ours was a very lively household! I always felt I'd rather have the children and their friends at our house; that way, I knew where they were. So we were the gathering house, especially when we lived in New York City. Before or after a school event, groups of children would come to our house to dress or sleep over.

We also had a foster child who lived with us for two years. This was another kind of learning experience for me. I was under the impression that if you gave a child enough love and the right atmosphere, you could bring him or her along in spite of an unfortunate background. But this child, at eleven years of age, had been in five different foster homes before she came to us. Her mother was an alcoholic.

Wanda couldn't take in love or give it back. The doctor near us said that it was most likely due to her liver being damaged from the alcohol her mother drank before her birth. I remember the first night she was with us. I was going to read her a bedtime story. She was eleven years old and she told me that no one had ever read her a bedtime story before. There were many joys and sorrows trying to integrate this little girl into our family. She did adjust to living in our family, but only to a certain extent.

We could bring her along only to a certain point because of her past experiences. This reinforced in me the importance of the early years of childhood. There are things we can't make up for later, things we can't get back. There are many techniques we can use therapeutically, but there are certain things from our early years that we cannot undo. These were important lessons for me to learn before I became a teacher. I learned a lot through that situation. They were not easy lessons.

My Work

When my own children were grown and off to university, my husband's work took us to California. This gave me the opportunity I had been hoping for. I enrolled in the teacher training program at the Waldorf Institute of Southern California and later accepted a position as an early childhood teacher at Highland Hall Waldorf School in Northridge, California.

Three years later we moved to Chicago. In the midst of my search for the next step as a Waldorf teacher, I met a person at a conference who offered a Waldorf-inspired home program. I returned from that meeting and realized I had a perfect place

Lunchtime at River Park Children's Garden

for such a program in my own home. The lower floor of our Chicago home became River Park Children's Garden, which I operated for eight years before coming to Great Oaks School in Evanston.

At Great Oaks School my work includes consulting, mentoring, teaching parent-child classes and serving on the Board of Directors. I also teach and mentor several students at Arcturus, the Chicago-based Waldorf Teacher Education program, where I teach early childhood classes for teachers and prospective teachers.

I am grateful that my career continues to evolve even in my sixties. It is out of my life experiences as a parent and teacher, and as a student of Rudolf Steiner and Anthroposophy, that I speak and write.

Our Children

It is my hope that this book will give parents insight into healthy child development, Waldorf education with its ideals and philosophy, and even the challenges of educating young children today and into the future. We have included the questions and comments of parents enrolled in the enrichment classes. Parents know the real questions to ask. Every day they earnestly work to give each of their children a healthy childhood. This is no easy task given the pace of the modern world and its distractions. The parents in my classes had such wonderful things to share! I think readers will feel a kinship with them as they read their comments and questions.

Today's children are pushed into early sophistication due to the influences of our culture: Barbie dolls, television, car rides that race children quickly past all the ads and store signs, impressions they take deeply into their beings.

But we cannot raise children in a vacuum, so we as parents have to pick and choose carefully what we expose them to in society. It has been said that what is normal today is not the same as

what is healthy. We must aim to have *healthy* children, protected in their early childhood from so-called normal experiences such as viewing violent television programs. Children absorb television messages and even billboard graphics through their sense impressions. Television can even affect eye and speech development. The passivity of watching television is at odds with the child's natural inclination to be active, to *do*.

Children take in everything from their environment

We must remember that our primary task with little children is to protect them and to provide good models for them to imitate. Children take into themselves everything they experience in the environment. Whatever is in the children's environment will be in them. Whatever is in them will affect their physical and spiritual growth. By positively affecting your children, you are beginning to impact your grandchildren's lives!

Following is an excerpt from a poem by Walt Whitman.[3] It inspired us as we wrote *Beyond the Rainbow Bridge* and illustrates so well that children actually become what is around them. We hope you will enjoy it as we did.

There Was a Child Went Forth

a poem from *Leaves of Grass* by Walt Whitman

There was a child went forth every day,
And the first object he look'd upon,
that object he became,
And that object became part of him
for the day or a certain part of the day,
Or for many years or stretching cycles of years . . .

[3] Walt Whitman, *Poem # 115, A Child Went Forth* in *The Oxford Book of American Verse,* selected and with an introduction by R. O. Matthiessen (New York, Oxford University Press, 1950), 276.

Raising Healthy, Happy, and Capable Children

I don't think there is anything that can match the joy that new parents feel upon welcoming their child into the world. In my experience, it is a feeling unlike any other. As we gaze at our new baby, another equally remarkable feeling rises to meet us. Like the Twelve Wise Women in Grimm's fairy tale, *Little Briar-Rose,* bestowing magic gifts upon the newborn princess, we suddenly find a longing in our hearts as deep and as poignant as our joy

Welcome to this world

is enlivening and exhilarating: we long to give our new baby the best life possible, to grant her good health, and a life's journey which allows her special gifts to unfold.

Then, perhaps a bit later, comes the third remarkable feeling: fear. For how are we to do this in the world in which we live today? How are we to find a pathway which truly offers our baby what she needs, and what we want for her?

Parental joy is a blessing and the longing that accompanies it is a guidepost for parents. Over the years, though, I have seen fear and uncertainty becoming stronger.

Out of my own experience as teacher, parent, and grandparent, I have found that three cornerstones can serve as trustworthy, bedrock foundations for raising healthy, happy, and capable children. The first is an understanding of children's development, for this teaches us to neither ask too much nor too little of our children as they grow. The second is an understanding of the importance of warmth for the growth and development of our children, to care for our children so that their bodies develop a strong capacity for warmth. And the third is an awareness of the gifts that life rhythms— daily, weekly, monthly, and yearly — bring to our children.

These are the three cornerstones for raising healthy children that I will be describing today.

Growing into Life

Babies take in their environment without discrimination. All impressions go deeply within: an infant takes in sound and color, feels how he is being handled and absorbs even the attitude of his mother as she cares for him. He absorbs all his surroundings as sense impressions, and is unable to judge or filter them. During this time, we must be the protective barriers for our babies.

According to Rudolf Steiner, infants' sense impressions "ripple, echo, and sound" throughout the whole of their bodies. From this perspective, what infants take in as impressions affects their life forces and thereby how their bodies develop and the ability of their organs to function rhythmically.[1] This remains the case particularly throughout the first seven years and most dramatically during infancy.

Birth to Two-and-a-Half Years

Let's imagine we are holding a tiny, newborn baby in our arms. What are our first impressions? Steiner noted that the life forces in an infant work mainly in the head, developing the nervous system. We can see that her head accounts for one fourth of her total length and is as broad as her whole chest; her jaw is small with a receding chin, and her features are rounded and soft. Her arms are short, and her pelvis and legs less developed than the rest of her body.

The newborn's organs are still developing both their structure and their ability to function rhythmically. You will notice that a new baby breathes unevenly. We can help our infants develop healthy inner rhythms by surrounding them with the repetitive rhythms of daily life. An infant's movements are also

[1] Rudolf Steiner, *The Essentials of Education*, Stuttgart, April 8–11, 1924, Lecture 2, trans. Jesse Darrell (London: Rudolf Steiner Press, 1926), 36.

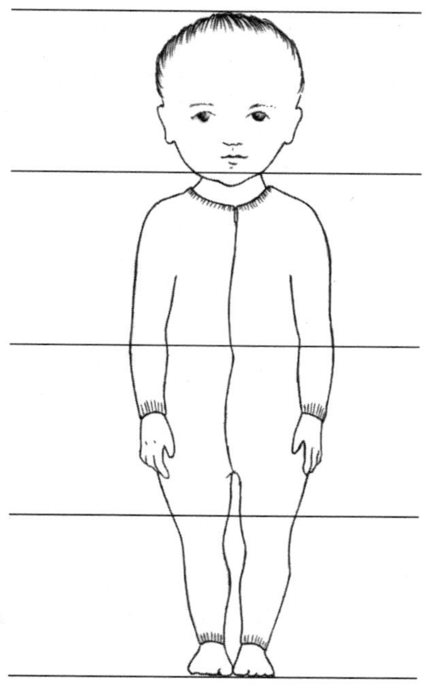

chaotic. If you watch a hungry baby, you will see tremendous activity and flailing of limbs. As babies adjust to their household's rhythms and begin to imitate adult movements, they gradually become more orderly in their own activity.[2]

During this first stage the most important achievements of the young child are in the areas of speaking, walking, and the more instinctive aspects of thinking. The infant begins this development as soon as he is born, for crying is the beginning of speech. As the infant develops, his speech evolves into that universal babbling we all know. Babbling is initially the same for babies all around the world. Soon this babbling differentiates into sounds ending in "ah" such as "mama," "ba ba," and "da da," then into sounds specific to the parents' language. He first names the people and objects in his surroundings and

[2] Freya Jaffke, "The Significance of Imitation and Example for the Development of the Will", *Waldorf Kindergarten Newsletter*, Spring, 1990, 1.

communicates with one-word sentences. Then, he adds verbs that bring these names into action. Finally, we hear simple, complete sentences and a sudden blossoming of more verbal interaction: our toddler seems to chatter all day long.

Something similar is happening in our baby's physical body. A newborn child cannot hold up her head without support, but gradually her neck grows strong enough to support her heavy head. Over the next few months, the infant begins to roll over and sit up, and to develop stronger arm and chest muscles. These early movements lay the foundation for walking.

As the legs and lower torso develop, the skill of crawling emerges. Movement and speech development are so interrelated that speech therapists often prescribe crawling exercises to help older children with speech difficulties.

It is quite wonderful to watch the development of a child in these first years of life. He tries over and over to accomplish the tasks of sitting, crawling, and walking. No matter how many times he falls down, he never gives up trying. An inner drive says, "I will do this!" A photo of my oldest granddaughter, so proudly finding her equilibrium in space, says this so well. In the picture, she is walking with both arms up in the air. She had let go of all other supports but was still holding on to heaven!

Still holding
on to heaven

Imitation plays a large role in speech development. If we speak well around children, they will also speak well. Steiner was among the first educators to ask us to refrain from using baby talk when speaking to young children, and to avoid correcting their speech. Simply speaking properly in the presence of the child leads to proper speech development.[3]

---

[3] Rudolf Steiner, "The Child Before the Seventh Year," in *Understanding Young Children: Extracts from Lectures by Rudolf Steiner Compiled for the Use of Kindergarten Teachers*, December 23, 1921 to January 7, 1922 (London: Anthroposophical Publishing Company, 1948), 1–7.

We can think back to our newborn baby who had two main activities — eating and sleeping. Then, we can follow her development during the first two years as she learns to sit, crawl, stand, and walk independently. She explores and discovers the world around her through movement and develops speech out of babbling.

We become aware that all these steps are part of our baby's awakening into the world. As our child moves through these ever-changing stages, we need to adjust our ways of relating to her.

Two-and-a-Half to Five Years

The main physical feature of this middle period of early childhood is observed in the growth of the torso. With this shift in growth, we see an emphasis on broadening and filling out of the trunk area, particularly the chest. Our child's life forces now work mainly in the upper chest area, primarily in the heart and lungs. As the trunk becomes the focal point of the child's growth, the proportion of head to total length changes to one-fifth. What we often call the "toddler tummy" is usually large and somewhat fatty looking, causing the whole torso to resemble an oval. Our toddler does not yet have a clear waistline or visible curve in the back.

What has become of the head in the meantime? Our toddler's chin has come somewhat forward, his upper lip protrudes

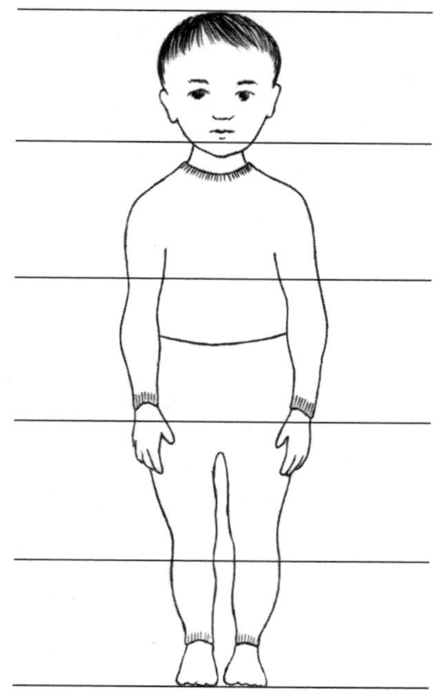

slightly over the lower lip, and his face has become more expressive. His neck has also grown longer. His legs and arms have both filled out more, though there is still no strong growth in the legs.

Our two-and-a-half to five-year-old's movements have become increasingly more agile and coordinated. She climbs everything and runs with ever-greater steadiness and speed, as any parent who has tried catching a runaway child will confirm.

We can also see a similar inner development. When our toddler is somewhere around two-and-a-half years of age, we begin to notice his developing memory. According to Steiner,[4] this early memory has its basis in imitation: "A child imitates

[4] Rudolf Steiner, *The Roots of Education*, Lecture 3, April 13-17, 1924 (London: Rudolf Steiner Press, 1968), 36.

something one day. The next day and the day following, he does it again, and the action is not only performed outwardly but also right into the innermost parts of his physical body. This is the basis of memory."

Children first develop an associative memory. Seeing a cookie tin will trigger the memory of taking cookies to Grandma. However, if you ask what she did that morning your toddler may not be able to recall the events. At the time, she may say she doesn't remember or may say very little. But sometime, days or even weeks later, some object or event will spark the child's memory, and a whole story will come flooding out in full detail. At this stage, it is best to refrain from asking children such questions because it places a demand on them that they are not ready for developmentally.

Around the age of three, a child begins to refer to himself as "I." Until then, he referred to himself as "me," or as his proper name, such as Tommy or Johnny. But one day a parent or teacher may hear, "I don't want to do what you want me to do. I want to do what I want to do."

Your child has reached a new stage. With this first experience of self as a separate being, thinking begins to awaken.[5] She develops a clearer sense of time—yesterday, today, tomorrow —

[5] Karl Koenig, *The First Three Years of the Child* (Spring Valley, NY: Anthroposophic Press, 1969), 48–49.

though it will be some time well in the future before she really understands what "We're leaving in five minutes" means. Her newly developed capacities of speech and memory are the basis for this awakening thinking. We used the example of the sight of the cookie tin sparking a memory of taking cookies to grandma's house. Gradually, a young child's memory becomes more independent and does not need visual cues to recall events or experiences.

Closely following the "I" stage is the "no" stage. Even if your son normally would want to do something you have asked him to do, he may now say "no." How we, the adults, react to that "no" is important. If we become flustered or reactive, our three-year-olds will imitate that. If it is time to wash hands, we should simply go with our child and both of us should wash our hands.

We must look a bit past the "no." Our toddlers are trying it on for size, as we would try on a pair of shoes. If we are not confrontational, both parent and child will be happier, though this doesn't mean backing off from a necessary task. But saying a rhyme, singing a song, or doing a task with your child will often bring the resistant will of the three-year-old along. A well-placed bit of humor works wonders during the "no" stage.

At approximately age three, children are able to express their feelings more readily and may now show more affection. Your child may crawl up on your lap for a hug in a way that didn't happen before. Children also develop more facility with language during this stage and begin to use adjectives to express how they feel about things. Earlier they may have asked for a cookie. Now, they may ask for a yummy chocolate cookie.

Another aspect of this stage of language development is the delightful use of made-up words. Our child plays with language in a very creative way and loves to listen to stories, especially at bedtime. This interest in stories grows out of and helps develop her expanding vocabulary and greater understanding of language.

This is also the age of "why." They will ask, "Why?" over and over but may not be very interested in our answers. They are exploring the fact that they can ask. It is a great temptation for adults to offer complete scientific answers in response. But a simple poetic answer is just fine and is really all they need at this stage. "Why is it dark outside?" "Father Sun is asleep now. He will come back in the morning to wake us up." For a child between three and five years of age, this is a fine explanation of the earth revolving around the sun.

Our youngster's social skills are also developing. He goes from the parallel play of the two-year-old to the interactive play of the three-, four-, and five-year-old. However, the "I" and "no" phases of the three-year-old are often followed by the well-known period of stubbornness around the age of four or four-and-a-half. When confronted or opposed, our four-year-old can really dig in his heels and be quite a challenge. As much as he enjoys playing with friends, sharing his toys can be hard for him. As he approaches the end of this stage, he enters a more harmonious period. Some educators have even referred to the five-year-old stage as a grace period.

Five to Seven Years

Between the ages of five and seven years, children undergo big changes in physical development, and we see a growth spurt particularly in the legs. Overnight the child seems to have outgrown all her clothes, especially long pants. At this age, the life forces mainly work in the limbs. The loss of the padding of baby fat makes muscles and joints more visible. The "toddler tummy" disappears with the slimming of her abdomen. The spinal column takes on a maturing curve and a defined waistline appears.

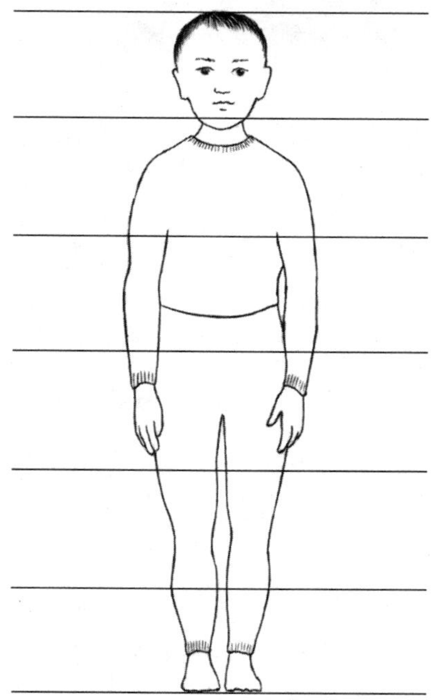

Play is more goal-oriented, more thought out, as the five-

Play dates with chosen friends become very important

to seven-year-old can now better direct his or her own actions. You can observe the purposeful run of a six-year-old as contrasted with the purely joyful run of a three-year-old. After repeated efforts, children acquire real skill on the climbing bars at the playground and want to show their newfound agility to whomever will watch.

Other changes we can see at this stage include greater memory development, which can make it more difficult for parents and teachers to distract children from inappropriate behavior:

now they remember what they wanted to do and will likely persist in trying to do it! Your child's sentences become more complex, and he may even shock you by using slang or swear words heard elsewhere. Expressions of sassy back talk as well as stronger bouts of anger over perceived injustices are all part of this transition period. The six-year-old is approaching school age and struggling to adjust to his newly developing capacities.

Our five- to seven-year-old grows much more aware of her relationships to peers. Play dates with chosen friends become very important. Her play world broadens from home and backyard to encompass the whole block. At dinnertime, parents now have to search in and around neighbors' homes for their child. Our older youngster now plays more sophisticated street games, with rules and shared equipment such as bicycles, jump ropes, balls, and chalk. She has a sense of freedom with her friends, but parents know they still need to keep a watchful eye.

The Importance of Warmth

Steiner taught that warmth supports life and is, therefore, a foundation of all health and development. We sense warmth even before birth, through the warmth of our mother's womb. As adults, we can generate our own warmth, but infants cannot do this very well. Babies must rely on their parents to provide body contact, proper clothing, and blankets to keep them warm. In many traditional cultures, mothers still swaddle their infants and keep their babies close to their bodies, especially during the first year.

Dr. Andrea Rentea, a physician practicing Anthroposophically extended medicine, explains, "A newborn who is shown around just after birth without being wrapped first for warmth, may end up in the incubator and need extra heat because he cannot maintain his own bodily heat."[6] It takes both care and effort to maintain warmth in a fragile infant.

Placing the newborn on the mother's abdomen at birth reinforces warmth by giving the infant some of the mother's own body heat. Likewise, oils such as calendula baby oil or almond oil support warmth. A baby who wears a hat and is swaddled after birth probably will be able to sustain his own warmth.

Toddlers playing on the cold floor need the good insulation of natural fiber rugs so that their legs don't lose warmth. In

---

[6] The Anthroposophical approach to healing is an extension of conventional medicine and is based on a comprehensive view of the human being as developed by Rudolf Steiner. Steiner's approach to the medical arts represents an integration of homeopathy, aromatherapy, naturopathy, vitalism, and Paracelsian medicine informed by his own insights and experience. Those interested in exploring this approach to healing may wish to read *An Introduction to Anthroposophic Medicine*, a collection of essays and lectures by Rudolf Steiner, published by Anthroposophic Press, 1999, Hudson, NY.

Europe, there is a folk saying that all the months with an "R" are months for babies to wear tights or long stockings made of wool or wool and silk. Seventy percent of a child's body heat is lost through the head, so hats become very important in maintaining warmth.

Pre-school children do not seem to know if they are feeling cold. If you ask them, they will usually say they are not cold, even though they may feel cold to the touch. They have not yet completely developed this inner sense. Dr. Rentea suggests that the child who has to expend her own energy to keep warm has fewer forces for growing a healthy body. This would also suggest that such a child would have less energy to devote to her overall development as well. We must protect her warmth by dressing her appropriately with natural fiber gloves, scarves, layers of clothing such as vests, tee shirts and sweaters. And what is more comforting to a child in the winter months than sitting by a warm stove, sipping a cup of time-tested hot fennel, chamomile, or rose hip tea, or warm, spiced apple cider? Spices such as marjoram, thyme, oregano, dill, and curries provide added warmth and flavor-enhancing qualities to a winter's meal.

It may surprise you to learn that childhood illnesses also support the development of a child's ability to sustain a healthy level of warmth. If you look at childhood illnesses, you will see that, unlike adult illnesses, they usually involve fever. Dr. Rentea's observation is that children who have had lots of fever illnesses in childhood grow up to be adults whose capacity for both soul and physical warmth is strong.

In a Waldorf early childhood classroom, we protect and nourish warmth by making sure that the children are dressed appropriately for the weather. In addition, we ask parents to provide a change of clothes and an extra sweatshirt or sweater for unexpected changes in the weather.

The Importance of Rhythm

When more people depended directly upon nature for their living, their lives were, of necessity, more rhythmic. They recognized that the rhythms of their days, their weeks, and even the seasons of the year supported them by yielding to them what they needed to live. Beyond that, they instinctively knew that these rhythms gave them added strength for their work, that they were good for people. Monday was wash day, Tuesday was ironing day, and so on, right through to the weekend, with Saturday being baking day, and Sunday set aside for church, visiting, and resting up for the new week. This routine gives children great security. I know that as a child I felt this in my life because my mother created these rhythms in our home. You'll find references to the chores of the week in children's songs and rhymes, such as *Here We Go 'Round the Mulberry Bush.*[7]

[7] See page 141.

Likewise, until quite recently, many people did their work to rhythmical songs. There were harvesting songs, rowing songs, songs about sawing wood. As people worked together to the rhythm of music, their tasks needed less individual strength. These songs enhanced the strength of the workers and made their jobs less stressful.

But if we look at our own lives, what has become of this rhythm? With automatic washers and dryers, we can throw in a load of wash any time, without regard to weekly rhythms. We may no longer have an ironing day, either. We can choose to iron just one item today, as needed, or avoid it altogether by purchasing clothes that don't need ironing. Children no longer see the tasks of daily life in a process from beginning to completion. None of us would like to give up our modern conveniences, but these rhythms did give children a sense of security and a sense that life had real form.

Margret Meyerkort, a retired English Waldorf kindergarten teacher, says that if children have regular external rhythms, then internal rhythms begin to develop for them as well. If dinner is at a regular time each day, the child's digestive juices will begin to flow as dinnertime approaches. If bedtime is regular, then children begin to feel drowsy as you are getting them ready for sleep, telling them a story, saying a prayer or verse. Their physical bodies and life forces adjust themselves to this routine.

Without the rhythms of life, our children feel like travelers to another time zone. If we jet across the ocean, we must compensate for the time change and the disturbances to our internal rhythms by becoming more self-aware. We would place our children in a similar state every day if we did not give them consistent rhythms at home. An arrhythmic home life can actually cut short a part of childhood by forcing a child to wake up too soon out of the dreamy consciousness of childhood. A child's energies can be stretched beyond her limits in an effort to maintain balance in a situation lacking in rhythm.

We all know that bodily rhythm is an indicator of health or illness. A doctor checks the patient's internal rhythms of heart, blood pressure, and pulse during an examination. When the patient has irregularities in these rhythms, these may indicate illness. Rhythms can also help maintain a person's strength: when a jogger is stopped momentarily by a red light, she will run in place while waiting for the light to change, not wishing to break her rhythm.

Some parents feel they cannot create rhythm for their children within their busy modern lives. Here, I remind parents that we all are born into a world of rhythms. These unconscious, cosmic rhythms can support us: the seven days of the week, the rising and setting of the sun, the phases of the moon, the changing of the seasons. We don't have to do anything to create these rhythms. They are a gift to us from the world of nature in which we live, and they can support us as we work to create rhythms for our children. When we provide supporting rhythms at home and school, we help our children connect in a stronger way with rhythms of nature.

Rhythms at School

In a Waldorf kindergarten classroom, these supportive rhythms are evident throughout the morning. We build into our schedule "breathing in" and "breathing out" times (or contracting and expanding times) to maintain a balance for the children which is neither boring nor over-stimulating. An example is our morning routine. First, there is a "breathing out" as the children arrive and have a short free playtime. Then, circle time follows as a "breathing in" or contracting activity where we come together to express our circle verses and songs through large and small movements. Afterward, the children "breathe out" again during the longer morning playtime and expand into their play. At clean-up and snack, they again "breathe in." As we play outside, they "breathe out" and finally, during our story and good-bye circle, they "breathe in" once more.

Rhythm is also a great aid to discipline. If children feel secure in knowing what is coming next, they are more willing to "go with the flow." An image of what is coming next in the day wells up within them to meet the outer activity brought by the teacher. When the children see the teachers putting away their own work and setting the tables for snack, they know it will soon be clean-up time. We put chairs in their appropriate places and start our tidying up.

We always put toys away in the same order. First, we put away larger pieces like play stands, and then large stumps of wood and wooden boards. Next we gather up things that belong in baskets or on shelves—seashells, stones, wooden figures, kitchen things. Lastly, we fold cloths and put them in baskets. As much as possible, we put things away in the same places every day, so our children soon learn where everything belongs and feel encouraged to help. All of this creates a classroom environment where children always know what to expect and are secure in the certainty that their needs will be met.

Rhythms at Home

We can carry these same rhythms into our homes and bring an awareness of this "breathing" quality as we arrange the activities of the day. We can plan our day at home with a young child so there is time to play outdoors, time to play inside, time to play with someone else, time to play alone, time to eat, and time to rest.

Gathering treasures from the back yard

Even in homes where both parents work, rhythm can become part of each day. You can establish regular routines for waking up and preparing for the day; you and your child can lay out her clothes the night before. Family breakfast and dinner become even more special if a child is going to school all day or is in a day care program. You might create a bedtime routine that could include sharing a little from each other's day, a story and goodnight verse. On weekends, try alternating relaxing times at home with more active outdoor play to create the breathing quality I mentioned earlier.

I am aware that some parents' workdays have irregular hours that would make even this schedule difficult to establish. The goal is to help the child have anchor points in each day and to work with each situation as creatively as possible.

Of course, this is more challenging when there are other children of different ages in the family. But you will find that even small rhythms that are part of the day's schedule will help your young child. Simple things like allowing children to set the table for supper at a certain time each day, perhaps with placemats and flowers, can change the whole atmosphere of the evening meal.

Marking the changing seasons within the year through particular activities brings seasonal rhythms into home life. For example, autumn, harvest time, is the kitchen time of year. It can be a time of canning and freezing. It can be a time of gathering in the harvest. Apple picking and peeling, preparing pies for baking are seasonal activities in which children can participate. It is a great time for gathering objects from nature. You can create a simple nature table from objects collected from outdoors: acorns, leaves, and special stones your children pick up on a walk. These are great treasures to children and connect them with what is going on in nature at that particular season.

The magic of candlelight

Celebrating the festivals at home can also delight your children. When they see you preparing for a certain holiday and taking out familiar decorations, children are filled with memories of the celebration from last year. These holiday celebrations give them confidence that wonderful, special times all come around again.

Each season has a special quality. When the outer light becomes dimmer as days grow shorter, we prepare for festivals such as

Hanukkah or Christmas that celebrate the strength of our inner light. Conversely, in summer we expand in the light and warmth, appreciating the dreamy quality of the season. Children take in deeply these special qualities of the changing year and are nourished by them.

Questions from Parents

Parent: I love to hear about how you were raised, Barbara, and I'm not surprised that you had a wonderful and rhythmic childhood. However, I grew up in a family of eight children with a mother who was harried. Life was crazy for her, and she was always doing laundry and running to catch up. I find myself doing the same thing in my own life. As an adult how can I catch that rhythmical sense and pass it on to my children? I can't seem to make it happen.

Parent: Me too! I feel chaotic inside and sometimes my needs are very different from those of my children. In the afternoons, I sometimes feel a need to get out of the house when the children might really need to be inside. How can I balance their needs and my own?

Barbara: I would start small. Take one aspect of your day and ask how you can make a beautiful rhythm out of that one activity. When you feel you have penetrated that activity with a new rhythm, select another one.

Parent: Could you give an example of this one activity?

Barbara: How about dishes? That's something we all do. Try to create a routine for the task. How do you clear the table? Become interested in the task at hand. Your children will take this in, too. Your attitude is so important. Are we rushing to get the dishes done or are we concentrating on one dish at a time?

Parent: My house is totally out of control. The children and I eat without my husband almost every night. We have dinner, then just leave the dishes. By then it's bedtime. I get the children in bed too late and go to sleep myself without getting the dishes done. When the house is in chaos, the next day the kids don't function as well, either. They don't seem to be able to get their play together.

Barbara: An earlier suppertime could make a big difference. This will give the children a little extra playtime while you clean up. And they will have a healthier digestion time before bed.

Parent: I always wonder if I am too rigid because I like beds made, dishes done. Am I too inflexible? However, what you are saying today is reinforcing that maybe I'm OK in trying to bring order. I have to deal with my own rhythms in order to meet my daughter's needs.

Parent: I know what you mean about dealing with your tasks while considering their rhythms too. It's difficult!

Barbara: It's always a juggling game isn't it? We need to find the middle point in such situations between rigidity and formlessness.

Parent: But if I do something they'd like to participate in themselves, we always have an explosive situation. Sometimes I can't do the planning ahead to have them help me or I feel, "Just let me do it fast, by myself!"

Parent: Sometimes I remember to get them working on a cookie sheet or on the floor to prevent the spilling of little beans or scraps of fabric. Then I can work with them present without them making a bigger mess to clean up afterwards.

Barbara: Including our children in our daily home tasks is a real art. Try thinking ahead of ways to do this so that you are prepared when the time comes. Your child's positive response will reward your effort.

Parent: At our house the days of the week have an irregular pattern. Every day is different. I teach one evening then the next afternoon. I'd like to figure out how they can know what we are doing each day. It would be nice if they knew what day we were going out, staying in, etc.

Barbara: We've discovered in our Early Childhood classes that children don't learn the days of the week by Monday, Tuesday, etc., but by "baking day" or "painting day". They learn by the activity they will do that day. Try to find one thing they can be involved in each day that identifies that day.

Parent: How about our pattern of pancakes on Saturday, eggs on Sunday?

Barbara: Yes, that's a way to identify the day for the children. Other ways might include bed changing day or the day the playroom is cleaned, and toys are sorted and ordered on the shelves.

Parent: I read a book a while ago about an Amish community. I was so touched by how this female character saw no drudgery or frenzy in this hard working life. The idea of setting the table was satisfying to her! My own two-year-old wants to help set the table all the time. I love to watch the simple beauty of her putting out the placemats. It makes me want to cry when I think of the times I didn't want her to help and just rushed to get the task done myself.

Parent: My mom had order. But there was no bending of this. It felt rigid at the time. However, I guess those rhythms are in me because I find I'm not happy without them in my life.

Barbara: That's a good point. We have to maintain a flexibility and receptivity to life and cannot hold wash day above all else. We must not become slaves to the schedule. But if we have a basic plan of what we'd like to do with our days, things go a lot smoother.

Parent: I have one child. God bless you moms with more! I don't know how you do it! Finding my rhythms sometimes depletes me by the afternoon. I'm feeling resentful and it's way before supper. There is no relief in sight from my husband. I'm not skillful at creating quiet time. I'm working on having my son be more independent at age three. I would like him to play alone sometimes. I really don't always want to sit and read to him.

Barbara: That's a very common problem. Then it is time to go outside. Change the scene. Get some fresh air.

Parent: How about having an eighth grade girl come in? Children love older kids.

Parent: But what if it's their nap time and they don't nap anymore and I'm tired?

Barbara: I used to tell my children that even if they weren't tired, I was, and they could play in their rooms for half an hour. That's all you need sometimes to feel a little bit freer. Or stretch out on the bed together and read a book.

Parent: Meals seem so all over the place for us. Our daughter isn't hungry at breakfast time. Our suppertime varies from 6 to 8 P.M. I feel a little guilty about it. Baths are late. Bedtime is then late, too. And the next morning is a holy terror as a result.

Barbara: At first try to shorten the time so there isn't a two-hour range you are dealing with in the supper hour. You may not be able to aim for 5:30 P.M. but how about between 5:30 and 7:00 P.M.? When this is in place, try shortening the range even more.

Parent: It helps me to plan dinner ahead in the morning. On busy days dinner will be a quick preparation of pre-cooked soup or a stir-fry. I use casseroles and my crock pot to speed things along in the evening.

Barbara: I hope everyone leaves today with new ideas for creating a rhythmic schedule in your life and the lives of your children. It can be a real challenge with all the distractions of everyday life, but the benefits for your family are well worth the effort involved.

Are there any further questions about the presentation this morning?

Parent: I'd like to go back to what you said earlier about children wearing hats. What about during the summer months?

Barbara: We believe children should wear hats even in warm weather. Children need about 20 minutes of sun per day for the vitamin D it provides for their bones, but Dr. Rentea believes that beyond this exposure, it is a mistake to be out in the direct unprotected sunlight between 10 A.M. and 2 P.M. All children regardless of skin color will have cumulative damage from the sun's rays, if over-exposed. There is definitely an increase in skin cancers linked to sun exposure and sunburn, regardless of the age at which they occurred.

Protection from the sun

Dr. Rentea says that the top of the head remains especially sensitive to the sun's rays, especially for the child younger than seven. We now have to protect our children from UV-B sun rays that cause sunburns and from UV-A radiation that damages the skin's underlying tissues. A wide brimmed hat protects the head and neck and also the eyes from reflected light. Dr. Rentea comments that in these times of a reduced ozone layer in the atmosphere, a hat protects the delicate fontanel covering the cerebral spinal fluid and the brain below it from environmental swings in temperature.

Play, The Lifeblood of a Healthy Childhood

When do children begin to play? What are their first toys? As I look back, I can remember my children first playing with their own hands; staring at them, moving them around in front of their faces and putting them in their mouths. Later, they could get a big toe in their mouths and play with a clean diaper left within reach. When they were a few months old they could grasp and shake a rattle. Small infants need very simple toys indeed.

Newborn to Two-and-a-Half Years

In addition to their own hands and feet, Rudolf Steiner felt that the most important toy for infants was a very simple doll. We can make such a doll in the image of the baby, that is, with a head one-fourth the entire body length, proportioned to the size of baby's own head.

This doll becomes a comforting companion for a young child. It is soft, cuddly and made from natural fibers. From Steiner's perspective, such a doll is an image of the human being. The child makes the doll a part of himself, so much so that sometimes a child will give his doll his own name. As the child gets older, we can make a doll similar to the early doll, but with arms and legs.[1]

[1] See page 152 for instructions.

While a child is learning to sit and stand upright and walk, he needs to imitate human beings. I encourage parents to give stuffed animal friends after a child has achieved the upright position of a human being. When we do give our children these toys to love and tend, we also take care that these animals have the same form and bearing as their living counterparts. The profoundly unconditional love of a child can redeem any animal or doll, but as parents and teachers we try not to place toys that are caricatures before our children. We want them to be able to offer their love to what is most real, and we do not want to risk having a caricature overpower the true image of an animal in our child's imagination.

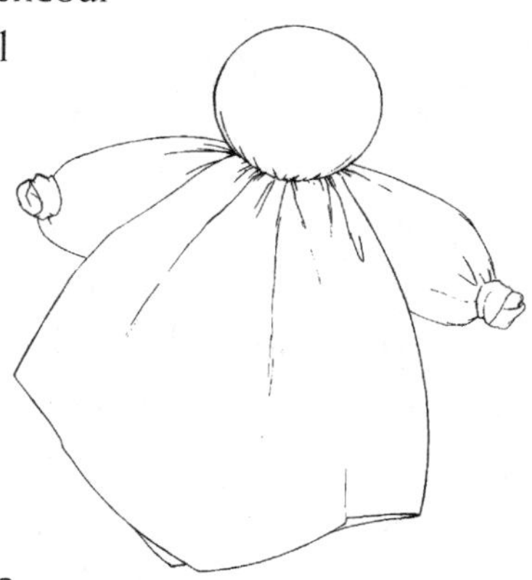

The toys we choose for our little ones are extremely important. With them children can play out what they experience every day. Small children do not need many toys. In fact, if they have too many toys in front of them, they may play with none of them. Other simple toys for toddlers include wooden spoons, pots, and bowls, which they will take out over and over again from the cabinets in the kitchen while a parent works nearby. A toddler prefers to play near us rather than in another room. Bringing orderly movements and concentration to our household tasks is important, especially in the presence of a young child. She will take in the total impression of our gestures and attitudes, and the efforts we expend at our work. She will imitate our work habits in her play and will also incorporate them into her developing attitudes towards work.

We may not be able to complete our tasks with a child around, but *how* we do our work is more important than *what* we accomplish. If we are only able to do fifteen minutes of concentrated work when a child is present, it will be fifteen minutes well spent.

Toddlers love to play with baskets that they fill and dump, fill and dump. The same is true with buckets of sand in sandboxes. They never tire of this play and will repeat it day after day. This is an extension of their own formative forces at work within their bodies. The filling and dumping relates to the organic processes of growth and metabolism, the building up and breaking down going on within these children.

Infants and toddlers have great fun splashing in the tub, sending water everywhere! They also love dropping food or spoons over the side of the high chair onto the floor and will repeat this over and over until the adult tires of picking them up. And they delight in crawling into a little space covered by a cloth, where they feel hidden away. This play is their way of learning about the world.

The way their toys are cared for is important for children. Toy boxes do not encourage putting toys away with care, even though they do encourage a fast clean up. And, be it ever so humble, a doll's "parent" is much happier placing the "baby" in a basket bed or little cradle for the night. Children find it easier to help clean up if they can put their toys away in the same place each day. Baskets for sorting and grouping toys, as well as shelves for arranging toys are aesthetically pleasing and make the room ready for the next day's play.

Two-and-a-Half to Five Years

Play is more focused at this time. Around three years of age, the first fantasy play appears—a wonderful stage of "make believe" and "let's pretend." This is a milestone in child development. Children of this age have the ability to transform their environment into what they need for their world of play. For them, reality and fantasy are interwoven; they cannot separate the two. The house built under the table becomes a real house for them.

How does this work? Young children absorb their surroundings as sense impressions. Their life forces are still so vibrant that these sense pictures continue to live within the child in such a way that the child re-experiences them fully. Then, he "joins in" with his experience, reenacting in his play bits and pieces or entire events that he has witnessed. Because his images are so alive, he needs only a simple table or toy to "be there." For young children, this is all very real.

If we adults wanted to copy someone else's actions as exactly, we would have to observe the person carefully over time and use our thinking to achieve the results we wanted. But a child instinctively takes in a scene as a whole picture and responds with an imitation that is more accurate than any adult could ever achieve.

Children at this age need toys they can transform as they play. In the pre-school/kindergarten we have such toys—baskets of shells, pine cones, wood, silk and cotton cloths, puppets. When children play with toys that can become something else as their play changes, they learn to work with and live in their environment. They

A doll is an image of the human being

actually "become" the shopkeeper, the farmer, and various professions of life. We have noticed they rarely want to play being a child their own age; a baby or an adult perhaps, but usually not someone their own age.

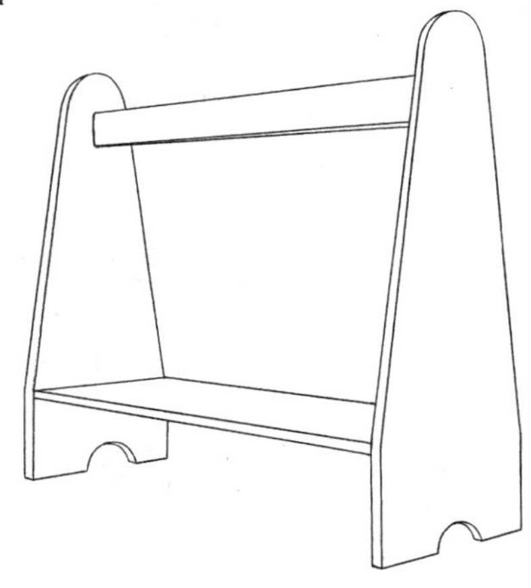

I remember the mother of a child in my class calling me in early December, not knowing what to buy her son for Christmas. She did not want to get her preschooler a video game or a plastic action figure, but she didn't know what else to get him. I suggested she buy several baskets and fill them with silks, crystals, wooden clothespins, and cotton cloths. In addition, I suggested she add two wooden play stands. She laughed, picturing how he would feel when he discovered that the neighborhood boys received computer games, and he got cloths. But that is what she bought for him. She reported later that it was a most wonderful Christmas. He and his younger sister played and played and were perfectly happy with these gifts.

It is important that children at this age be given a space in the day to play without interruptions. This allows them to fully play out life's roles and to develop concentration. They will play out of the strength you have given them through devotion to your adult work, not necessarily because you sat down to play with them, though that is fine, too, sometimes. This is helpful to remember as we approach our daily tasks. Our children are observing us instinctively, as we move through even the most mundane household tasks.

It is good if we can give our children experiences with the four elements of earth, water, air, and fire. Supervised playing with the elements connects children with the natural world and anchors them gently to earth. It also strengthens their life forces by allowing them to create entire worlds out of the raw materials that form their own bodies. Earth play is making mud pies, playing in the sandbox and in the soil. All children love water play—washing dishes, making foam in the water with an eggbeater, and gathering boats and kitchen containers into the tub for a bath at the end of the day. Air play includes toy parachute and airplane tossing, blowing seed pods and dandelion puffs, and even blowing bubbles into the wind. All experiences with fire need adult supervision. A few examples of ways to bring this element to your children are gathering with friends for a midsummer bonfire, enjoying a winter fire in the fireplace or wood stove, or burning candles on the dinner table.

Once I took the children in my class outside after it had been raining for days. The ground was quite saturated, and we discovered earthworms on the sidewalk. The children wanted to save the earthworms from being stepped on or drowning and proceeded to spend their entire outside time moving the worms one by one from the sidewalk to resting places under the trees. This sort of creative activity calls upon the living formative forces within them and extends it into the surrounding world. You can think of it as exercising life itself: the strength a child can gain from this can serve him his entire life.

Creative play involves growth and development; it will not be the same tomorrow. Tomorrow will be a new day, and play will move in a different direction. This is why we generally don't let children save the houses and trains and villages they have made in the classroom.

Remember to allow enough time for tidying up to be fun, too. No child or adult likes drudgery. We had the idea of "clean-up boards" in our kindergarten. Some children would place toys on the boards and then the "delivery people" would slide them into their proper locations.

You usually don't gain much by saying to young children, "Go clean up your room." That is too overwhelming. But you can say, "Come, let's put our toys away for the day. You may have a basket and help, too." If they resist at first, be happy if they do just a few things. You can build on this experience the next time.

Five to Seven Years

Playtime is much more harmonious at this age. By this time, children have usually learned to share toys. Five-year-olds are at the peak of creative play and have a longer concentration span. It is a real grace period for parents and teachers. Five-year-old play is also more sophisticated. Children are involved in the building, or growth process of play, rather than in the final product. For example, they may spend considerable time setting the stage for playing "bride and groom." One group got so involved in creating a book for the minister to use at the wedding that they never actually had a wedding ceremony. Yet, at the end of playtime, they felt satisfied with the process. "Doctor's office" play is similar. Children at this age will look around to see what they may use for the doctor's office and set up an elaborate waiting room and equipment for splints, casts, and crutches. They may or may not get around to actually seeing "patients."

If children are engaged in puppet play, they now want an audience for their shows and are no longer content to just play with the puppets. When setting up a puppet show, they often gather chairs for the audience even before setting up the scenery.

Play is more thought out at this age. If the five- to six-year-olds are painting, their thinking processes will be part of the activity. Before beginning, a five-year-old will think about what to paint, whereas the three-year-old will just dive into painting for the pure joy of experiencing the colors.

Children at this age will want a more detailed doll to dress and undress, with a knitted or cloth body, arms, legs, and even a few stitches for eyes. Long doll hair that can be brushed, braided or formed into a ponytail is lots of fun for little girls, especially.

One day the teacher may hear from a six-year-old, "I'm bored." This remark usually indicates the child is in the midst of what we call the "six-year-old change," otherwise known as "little puberty." A big change is now taking place within. Previously, the toys in her environment stimulated her play. Now her inner world inspires her creative play, and she can pick and choose which toys she needs. The six-year-old will often sit with her friends at the beginning of playtime to talk about what to play that day. Then they will search the room for objects to transform into what they need.

"I'm bored," really means that a child has not yet figured out how to use this new inner capacity. He does not know what to do with his new feelings and awareness. When we see older children going through this change in the classroom, we involve them in our adult work: peeling fruit, sanding wooden toys, or sewing a puppet, for example. This lets them experience the individuality of an adult engaged in purposeful work. The result of this is that imaginative pictures gradually begin to arise within the child. One day he will run off with a new idea and be able to play again. It is important to let children go through this process, whether it takes days, weeks, or months.

Children at this age are more dexterous than before, and we should take this into consideration when we select toys for them. Their formative forces now concentrate in their limbs; they are able to finger knit[2] with more success and less frustration. The simple toys and crafts such as we find in a Waldorf

[2] See page 163 for instructions.

classroom engage not only the developing dexterity of five- to seven-year-olds, but also their imaginations. This is something that neither battery operated toys nor highly detailed technical toys can do.

Boys at this stage do tend to look for more technical playthings. We don't have technical toys in our early childhood classrooms. However, children can create technical toys out of simple things we do have. Once in my classroom, the boys wanted to make a train. They used a rocking chair for the engineer's seat. Other children gathered around the rocker, throwing little black river stones under the rocker as fuel to fire up the train. Similarly, one five-year-old boy found a lady's lace scarf in the room, tied it around his waist, and turned it into a

tool apron. He filled the apron with tools, became the repairman, and asked the other children what they had that needed repair that day.

In the same vein, these five- to seven-year-olds begin asking more philosophical questions, so we might think they are looking for more scientific answers. However, answers grounded in technology and science can overwhelm children with too much information. Too early an intellectual approach may leave them feeling stymied. To understand intricate technical or philosophical relationships, human beings must first picture them. The force that enables us to create mental pictures is the same life force that forms our organs as young children. If we place intellectual demands on children too early, we interfere with this force and may compromise the child's health.

Just as creative, imaginative play gives children a healthy relationship to life, it is also true that children create their play to the extent that they are healthy. In this regard, I feel I need to say that I believe television is the greatest hindrance to play today. Watching television is a passive activity: children don't have to bring anything out of themselves to have the experience. A child's imagination atrophies like an unused muscle if it doesn't get a daily workout. They take in the images of television very deeply, but these images are not part of their own life, their own reality. In my observation, children cannot build up a play situation out of television images; they can only reenact what they have seen on the screen.

Parents have commented to me that their children sometimes act "wired" after watching television or playing video games. To me it looks like the children's will energy has been held back like a river behind a dam. Eventually, the "dam" bursts and the children's energy explodes.

I have also noticed over the years that children who watch television or videotapes for more than an hour and a half per week will play television characters at school. Their imagination has been stunted for the more creative play that arises out of real life imitation. I would ask all parents to consider these things.

Children as the Creators of Play

Author Joseph Chilton Pearce has said, "... all children want to do is learn, which they try to do through their greatest learning tool, play."[3] We, as parents and teachers, must allow children to develop at their own pace, unhindered by academic information pouring in to them from all sides. Today's children have more and more things to play with but they can *do* less and less with these toys. Children can play during their

[3] Joseph Chilton Pearce, "Child's Play". Newsletter of the *Suncoast Waldorf Association*, Fall 1993.

early years only if their parents understand their needs and support them by providing appropriate play spaces and toys at home.

The child is the creator of play at a Waldorf school. Children play from the images created during circle time and story time, and from the images of their own life experiences. If there are rich images around the children, they can create satisfying and appropriate play.

I'd like to describe the environment of a Waldorf early childhood, or kindergarten, classroom in more detail. A nature table, usually centrally located in the room, reflects the changing seasons and helps the children connect with what is happening in the natural world around them. The walls of the room are painted with soft colors, usually a light peachy-pink, and there may be sheer cloth at the windows to diffuse and soften the light from outside. There are a minimum of posters and pictures on the walls so children can focus on their play without distraction.

Toys in a Waldorf kindergarten are not what we usually find in other preschools. As was described earlier, there are baskets holding seashells, pine cones, cloths, sections of logs and simple natural-fiber dolls and puppets. Instead of desks for reading and writing, we see a little housekeeping area where the doll family lives. A table and chairs, some dishes and cooking utensils, a stove, a doll high chair, and dolls stimulate play imitative of the life our children experience at home.

Our dolls are simple cloth dolls with a minimum of details. The child's imagination can inwardly complete these details and change them according to whether he needs the "baby" to be happy, sad, ill, or healthy that day. A wood building area with baskets of irregular blocks of wood cut from tree branches, some wooden stumps, and carved wooden animals and people becomes the scene for villages, trains and farms. The dress-up basket, cotton capes, and felt crowns provide the necessary ingredients for dramatic play. A puppet table with simple table puppets, cotton and silk cloth for setting the scene, and baskets of shells and stones encourage children to create their own puppet shows for each other, imitating puppet shows and stories the teachers present as part of the curriculum.

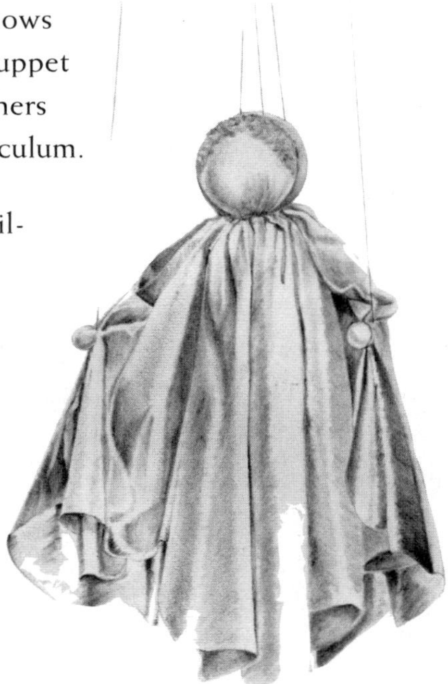

New parents often ask if children know how to play with these things. These are toys with magic still in them. Children have to work to find that magic and bring it out in play. Each day, play time is a time of transformation. The sections of logs, for example, now form a village. Later, the same logs might be used for telephone play. The seashells are pretend money for shoppers but later become pretend food for children who are playing restaurant.

When problems arise during playtime, the children try to resolve them. For example, a roof may have collapsed on a house built of wooden play stands, cotton cloth, and clothespins. The children may express different points of view on how to repair it. Some will declare the house is too small for all the children who want to play inside and announce that it must be enlarged. These children must then arrive at a compromise with those who want it left as it is.

Through these interactive experiences, children develop faculties they will need later in life. They may be able to approach problem solving from many different sides as a result of the many opportunities provided by this creative play.

The richness and health-bringing qualities of such an environment for children are obvious. You can bring these qualities into your home as well, thereby giving your children wonderful resources they can use to grow into healthy, happy, and capable adults.

Questions from Parents

Parent: What about an active boy? My son has no interest in dolls or doll play.

Barbara: Even if your son has no interest in playing with dolls, it is still important to have a "little prince" in his bed as a sleeping companion. The doll can be incorporated into what you and your child are doing during the day. At bedtime the "little prince" can join you as you read a story to your child. You may find, though, that you'll have to introduce the doll into play and find ways to bring it to life for your little boy.

Parent: But what about a two-year-old boy who wants things that move and roll?

Barbara: An active child can be just as active with the toys I have described—dumping baskets, making houses with cloths and clothes pins, building towers. An active child will play with these same toys in a more active way. I don't think we need to change the toys, but do include outside play as often as possible. Outside activity is especially important for more active children.

Parent: I used to believe in nurture over nature, but that was before I had a son. The boys in our park can turn sticks into guns. We don't have guns at home, but boys seem to want to shoot things! If I always stopped my son from shooting, I'd be on his case all the time.

Barbara: It is the toys in the home that speak the loudest message to your child. If guns aren't in the house, that message is clear. If boys are hurting others with sticks, then the sticks have to go down on the ground. Working with a more positive approach, however, one could help the children gather the sticks for a bonfire or build something for their play. Then, you will have shown what they may do with sticks.

Parent: I'm trying to undo what I have done by providing too many plastic and battery toys. Is it too late to get rid of these toys?

Barbara: You'll have to do it gradually and maybe even have to show them how to use more simple toys in their play.

Parent: What do you do about the toys that relatives give your kid? Lots of relatives want to give something they can buy, not order. Lots of it is plastic and the quantity is staggering.

Barbara: How about making a list well in advance of the holiday with suggestions that are appropriate? Otherwise, sort and pack away some of the toys for rainy days.

Parent: Are there degrees of watching television?

Barbara: How much poison is best? None, of course. But total abstinence may be antisocial and unrealistic. Monitoring the content and setting limits are probably more workable options. This amount varies with different children. Watch their play and listen to their conversations. If you hear and see too much television play then you need to cut back even more. If we can maintain these guidelines at home with our children, we are truly giving our children a great gift.

Parent: What about those smooth log sections we see in the Waldorf early childhood classrooms? Where do you find those?

Barbara: We just go out in the woods and find a thick branch or stump of a tree. Then there is wonderful work to be done with the children in smoothing the cut log pieces with sandpaper. They become even more interested in these toys if they have been allowed to help create them.

Parent: What about the puppets in the classroom? How are those made?

Barbara: The stand-up puppets are simply a head and a rectangular piece of felt sewed up the back and stuffed with wool. Fleece for hair and a simple cape or apron create a character for a story.[4]

Parent: My children are involved with after school classes and organized sports. Isn't this playtime, too?

---

[4] See page 159 for instructions.

Barbara: Sometimes parents fill their children's afternoons with activities, such as team sports, ballet, music lessons, etc. It is important to remember that I'm talking about "free play" experiences. Parents need to make time for children to have unstructured play time.

Parent: Could you also address the use of books with little children?

Barbara: There is a lot I could say about books.[5] But basically, children love to be read to and love to hear stories told to them. It is good to have some books with pictures and some without. Children like the opportunity to picture their own scenes, to do their own internal imaging. At night, don't read too many books in a row before bedtime because there will be too many images in their heads. It can give children a kind of mental indigestion that they take into their sleep. It is very rewarding to alternate story reading with storytelling, either from your own adventures as a child or from a tale you have taken the time to memorize.

Parent: When you discuss the work of parents at home, you don't mean my work at the computer, do you?

---

[5] See Recommendations for Further Reading.

Barbara: No, I am referring to housework. However, we should bring the same concentration to our housework as we do to our paperwork or computer work. That is what your child takes in and will bring out again in play. That is how it works. They take in your gestures and attitudes. It's rather mystical and scary how much children absorb from us.

Parent: There is a limit to how much housework I can get done before I must stop. The children don't want me to work for long.

Barbara: Getting them involved in some aspect of your housework will help. If you have a toddler, for example, give her a metal bowl with a little water in it and a sponge. While you are wiping the stove or counter tops in the kitchen she may clean, too. When you sweep the kitchen floor, let her use the hand brush and dust pan. She may even manage to actually sweep up the little pile of dust you have gathered together. Toddlers are not usually able to happily entertain themselves in another room for very long so you'll need to be creative in finding ways to keep your child engaged while you work.

Parent: What about the interactions between parents and children? Were you telling us not to play with our children?

Barbara: I'm not saying don't play with your children, but adults should interfere as little as possible with their play because whatever the adult brings to the play comes from intellectual adult thinking, not from the children's creative imitation. Just sitting next to them while you do your mending is often enough to make them feel that you are there with them and participating in what they are doing.

Developing a Child's Twelve Senses

Close your eyes for a moment and think back to the birth of one of your children. When your baby was born, you probably first heard her cry, then you saw her and instinctively reached out to touch and hold her. You spoke softly, welcoming her to earth. In this way, you stimulated your child's senses from the first moments of birth.

The infant enters the world through three doors: breathing, nutrition, and sense impressions. Adults can ward off

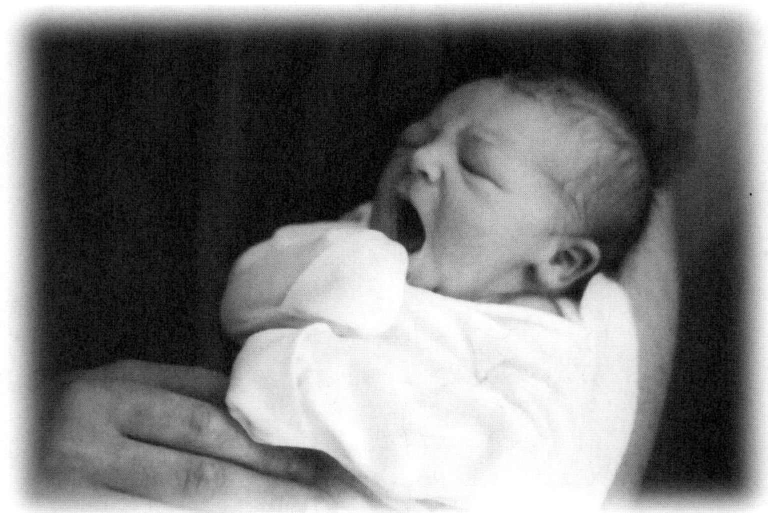

Protecting an infant

unpleasant sense impressions. Our powers of thinking and judging can help us erect inner barriers against impressions that are too loud, unpleasant, or harmful. Young children cannot erect such protective barriers within themselves. Children trust the world completely and absorb each and every impression with great openness.

From birth to age seven a child's forces are primarily devoted to building up her physical body. By seven, these formative forces have changed every cell in her body. From the perspective of Steiner and of Waldorf education, the sense impressions she absorbs can so strongly influence these forces that they make the difference between a strong healthy body or a body that may be prone to chronic illness later in life. In this chapter, we will look at our human senses as characterized by Rudolf Steiner and explore why Waldorf early childhood teachers strive to protect and nourish them.

Steiner spoke of twelve senses. At the time he was making his observations and determining how best to characterize the sensory capacities of human beings, it had not yet occurred to anyone that *five* was the only possible number of senses. During his time, the number of human senses was characterized differently depending upon who was discussing them and the most common numbers were five, six, seven, ten, and eleven. Steiner himself began his work by characterizing ten physical senses and three supersensible ones. Later, he determined that a more accurate, effective, and useful approach was to view the human being as having twelve senses which integrate the capacities of body, soul, and spirit. In other words, the five senses we learned about in school are not the only way to accurately view the human being, and may not necessarily be the most useful approach.

Dr. Albert Soesman has given a thorough account of Steiner's description in his book, *The Twelve Senses*.[1] Steiner divided the

---

[1] Albert Soesman, *The Twelve Senses*, trans. Jakob M. Cornelis (Stroud, England: Hawthorne Press, 1990).

twelve senses into three groups: the will senses, the feeling senses and the cognitive senses. The will senses, or physical senses directed primarily at one's own body, are touch, life, movement, and balance. The feeling senses, those used mainly to establish the relationship of the human being to the world, are smell, taste, sight, and warmth. The cognitive senses, directed toward the inner experience of both self and others, are the senses of hearing, speech, another's thought and another's "I". When we understand all twelve senses, we can clearly appreciate the importance of protecting and nourishing them, especially in the early years of life.

WILL SENSES	FEELING SENSES	COGNITIVE SENSES
Physical Senses (Directed at own physical body)	Soul Senses (Relation of man to the world)	Spiritual/Social Senses (Directed inward)
Touch	Smell	Hearing
Life	Taste	Speech
Movement	Sight	Another's Thought
Balance	Warmth	Another's "I"

Will Senses

The Sense of Touch

Close your eyes and touch the surface of the chair on which you are sitting. Move your hand around a bit, exert a little pressure, and be aware of the many impressions you are receiving through your sense of touch. You will be aware of temperature, texture, resistance, friction, moisture, dryness, and more. Your sense of touch tells you something about the object you are touching, and it tells you something about your own boundaries.

What I touch
also touches me

Children become aware of their boundaries daily as they grow from babies sucking on their hands into toddlers bumping into things as they explore the house. They want to touch everything, and it is painful for them if not allowed to do so. During these early years, it is best to remove valuable figurines or unsafe objects so your small child can freely touch things within reach.

What children touch and what touches them is important. In a Waldorf early childhood program, toys are made of natural materials, such as wool, cotton, wood and silk. Each of these has something unique to teach children about the world around them. If at all possible, we recommend that you dress your children in natural fibers, which keep children more comfortable in hot and cold weather.

We see that touching has a two-fold aspect, separating and connecting. Touching tells a child something about himself; it enhances his sense of himself. Whatever I touch also touches me. Through touching, children can feel a loving connection to their environment. At the same time, they feel the separations or boundaries between themselves and other persons or objects. These experiences — separating from and connecting with another — gradually awaken the child to the experience and value of relationships. As I touch you, I understand your being more fully. As I touch the chair, I understand the nature of a chair more completely. Through developing a healthy sense of touch, an understanding for these boundaries gradually develops.

The Sense of Life

This inner sense allows us to experience our own constitution, to know whether we feel well or not. Through this sense, we monitor how we are at any given time and determine the meaning of our aches and pains. For little children, hunger or thirst is a type of pain. This pain teaches them what their bodies need. Their sense of life carries impressions of well-being or danger to their awareness.

Parents frequently express concern about violent, even bloody incidents that occur in Grimm's fairy tales. Today, we often see these tales edited to remove or soften these aspects. This results in a kind of deprivation of our children's sense of life that is similar to the effects of painkillers and can dull that sense. At a Waldorf school, these unedited fairy tales are an important part of the curriculum of early childhood and first grade.

In a true fairy tale, such as those collected by the Brothers Grimm, human beings undergo trials and suffering and accept that deeds are a part of proving oneself worthy of the reward at the end of the path, whether the reward is the hand of the princess or a kingdom. They confront evil and overcome it.

Children experience the greed of the wolf and the evil of the witch quite differently than we adults do. They experience these qualities more as archetypal pictures about life, but do not yet identify themselves personally with the suffering. They trust that there will be a happy ending or that good will triumph over evil.

Such stories strengthen the moral lives of children, so that later, after these pictures have lived in them for many years as seeds, this strength and guidance will help them to deal with the challenges life brings to them. They will be better able to face the nature of greed, evil, or jealousy in themselves and the world around them. We all know that we learn more from our pain and difficulties than from our joys. Soesman noted that human beings would never be able to develop if they could not feel pain. When we change the classic fairy tales to soften what we perceive as violence, we rob children of this morally strengthening experience. If the teacher tells stories in an objective way, without dramatizing the so-called scary parts, the stories do not frighten the children.

A true fairy tale contains a balance of joy and sorrow. Children experience this right into their bodily constitution. A fairy tale stimulates and nourishes their sense of life if the tale is told without editing and without vocal dramatization. The art of telling a fairy tale is to tell it completely and calmly, as though you were describing a flower in your garden.

When the challenges of a fairy tale resolve at the end of the story, early childhood teachers often see and hear the children sigh with relief—evil has been overcome, justice has been done. We know then that the children's sense of life has been exercised in a way that fosters healthy development.

We do, however, determine which fairy tales are age-appropriate by the way evil is depicted and by the complexity of the story.[2] A Waldorf early childhood teacher can help you make this determination if you have a question about a specific tale you wish to read or retell to your children.

The Sense of Movement

This sense gives us awareness of our muscles and joints when we move them. For example, if you bend your elbow, you will have a sense of muscles in the arm contracting and expanding. This sense also gives us an awareness of our movement through the space around us. The child learns to sit, stand, and move about at her own pace through developing this sense.

We don't recommend using baby walkers or springy jumping seats hung from doorways. A child naturally exercises and strengthens the forces of his will through achieving an upright position when he is ready. Soesman says that forcing a child

---

[2] See page 148 for list of age-appropriate fairy tales and stories.

Practicing her new crawling skills

into these positions too early by using walkers puts an unhealthy strain on immature joints and muscles and, in addition, may compromise the development of his sense of movement. These devices, in effect, tell the child's body it is able to make these movements in spite of the fact that without these devices it could not do so.

Many children at Waldorf schools are fortunate to participate in eurythmy classes, an art form that encourages healthy movement. In eurythmy, the children experience a harmony between their physical and etheric bodies as they move to music or poems. In the early childhood classes this sense is nourished and stimulated through movement at circle time as well as indoor and outdoor play.

The Sense of Balance

In our ear, we have three semicircular canals at 90 degrees to one another. This formation allows us to have a relationship with the three dimensions of space; with objects above and below, to the right and left, in front and in back of us. Many of us have experienced the inner ear's relationship to balance. Did you ever have an ear infection and feel woozy and off center? An ear infection creates an inner restlessness in us. I believe this feeling must approximate what a child would feel if he learned to walk before he was developmentally ready.

We must allow the sense of balance to develop as a normal process out of a child's readiness. Let the child's inner drive encourage him to try over and over to stand and eventually walk unassisted. If we prematurely put an infant into an upright position or use walkers and jump seats, we prevent him from experiencing the step-by-step struggle in developing this sense as well.

I once boiled it down into a few words for a first-time mom. I told her that if it isn't something her child can do on her own, then it is too soon for her or not the right activity. Take your

cues from your child. If she shows a readiness for a new activity, such as sitting or standing alone, then she is ready for it.

Many children's games foster a healthy development of this sense. In a Waldorf early childhood class, we walk the balance beam, jump rope, and, at circle time, hop, skip, and go up on our toes as we gesture and move to our poems, nursery rhymes, and seasonal songs. All of these activities exercise and develop a young child's sense of balance.

Feeling Senses

The Sense of Smell

Through this sense we experience the quality of things—sweet chocolate, sour pickles, spoiled food — and our very personal relationship to them. We cannot hold our breath for very long, so even as adults we are limited in how long we can block out these sense impressions. We experience scents in a very individual way. For example, some of us find the fragrance of hyacinths very pleasing while others cannot tolerate it.

Smelling is related to memory. If we walk into a home where apple pie is baking, we might remember grandmother's wonderful pies from childhood. Smelling the pines as we walk in the woods may remind us of having walked over pine needles in the woods as children. There can be painful memories, such as having tramped in dog dirt, attached to offensive smells. In my home, we once had a refrigerator that quit working while we were away on vacation. We returned to find that all the food in the refrigerator had spoiled while we were gone. In spite of a friend's efforts to clean the refrigerator before we returned home, that awful smell lingered inside the refrigerator for months afterward. Every time we opened it, we remembered coming home from vacation that day.

It is important to remember that children are very sensitive to the many strong aromas around them. Many products, from soaps and shampoos to cleaning supplies and laundry detergents, are scented. Everything that the child takes in from her environment in these formative years, including scents, is taken up by the etheric body and used to build the child's physical body. Our adult sense of smell is much duller than a child's, and the onslaught of scents we deal with everyday affects us differently than it does a child. Our bodies have already been formed and are not so deeply affected by what we take in from our environment.

If we have good scents around us, our whole body responds, and we tend to open up to them. We deliberately include the wonderful aromas of cooking rice or apples or bread when we make snacks in a Waldorf kindergarten. Children respond to these scents, and their digestive juices begin to flow.

If, on the other hand, the child's environment consistently presents him with unpleasant odors, then he may tend to close up and not develop his ability to open trustingly to the world around him. This has obvious implications for later social development.

The Sense of Taste

Digestion begins in the mouth. The sense of taste begins the process of uniting us with matter as we chew and swallow our food, which will then become a part of us in a substantial way. Different areas of the tongue are attuned to different qualities of food. The back of the tongue senses bitterness; the front, sweetness; and the sides, salty and sour flavors. Soesman pointed out that these different qualities each have different effects, especially on children who are more sensitive to them. Sour and salty foods have a positive awakening effect on an overly dreamy child while sweets create a sense of well-being for the sad child. Bitter foods engage the will of the unmotivated child. Soesman says we can use these insights to work therapeutically with constitutional imbalances.

Our sense of taste should teach us what is good for us to eat. Whenever possible, we recommend organic fruits and vegetables, especially for children. By offering the child a wide variety of tastes, unaltered to suit adult preferences, we stimulate a child's healthy development. The overuse of salt, sugar, and artificial flavorings may distort the relationship between our bodily needs for certain foods and our sense of taste.

The Sense of Sight

Through the sense of sight we experience light, darkness, and colors. In *The Foundations of Human Experience,*[3] Steiner quotes from Plato to explain that in the process of seeing, our eyes stretch forth their vision like a pair of arms, extending and grasping the perception.

Soesman describes an experiment where three panels were placed before a subject. Two panels were orange with a gray panel placed between them. The gray panel had a black dot in the middle of it. The subject first focused on the black dot and then the panels were taken away. The subject saw an

3 Rudolf Steiner. *The Foundations of Human Experience*, Lecture 3 (Hudson, NY: Anthroposophic Press, 1997), 66–67.

orange after-image where the gray panel had been, and a blue after-image where the orange panels had been. One thing this experiment tells us is that we inwardly transform our eyes' perception of color so that we experience inwardly the color that is complimentary of the objective color we perceive.

Since the inner experience of color is much stronger in children, we can use it therapeutically. If we dress a withdrawn child in blue, she will feel the liveliness of the blue compliment, orange. Red overalls on a hyperactive child will help her feel the quietness of the compliment, green.

The experiment also points to the importance of resting places for the eye, where we can inwardly recreate what we have seen. In the Waldorf early childhood classroom, therefore, we do not decorate the walls with many pictures and posters. Some wall space is left open where our vision can rest, free of over-stimulating images.

We want the child's inner color experience to be as true and pure as possible. Therefore, we take care to use colors that are not harsh or over-stimulating. Walls in the classroom are often painted a soft peach color. We prefer natural daylight filtered through sheer gauze curtains to soften the light.

In our activities we also use color to help develop a healthy sense of sight. We use watercolor paints with children instead

Children experience color radiating through light

of tempera paints. The qualities of the paints are very different. With watercolors children experience light radiating through color, whereas with opaque tempera paints, they experience light reflected from color. We also prefer using crayons and modeling wax which contain pure beeswax because the colors are more rich.

Our puppet show scenery displays colored silk or cotton cloths. These natural fabrics reflect the light very differently than synthetic materials, and thus enhance the child's color experience. This helps to stimulate a healthy development of the sense of sight.

The Sense of Warmth

In Chapter Four of *The Twelve Senses*, Soesman refers to the two-fold nature of the warmth, or temperature sense, as he calls it. In the first instance, he gives an example of how we experience the effects of warm or cold temperatures on our body and react accordingly. Our bodies relax in warm temperatures, tense and contract in cold ones. We take off or add clothing as needed to maintain our ideal body temperature. As we discussed before, it is very important that we parents and teachers nourish a child's physical warmth.

But we also experience soul warmth or coldness coming towards us from other human beings. We open ourselves through interest in making contact with someone. Then we feel the reaction that comes from him. A young child is much more sensitive than we adults are to the soul responses from those around him. Is it a cold reaction that causes him to back off and maybe even withdraw into himself, or is it a warm friendly reaction that fills him with enthusiasm and stimulates further interchange?

In a Waldorf early childhood class, the soul warmth that Soesman refers to is fostered between the teacher and each individual child as well as among the group as a whole, including the children's parents. This is an important aspect

Children enjoy washing dishes after snack time

of our work with young children. The children also learn that we are stewards of our environment. They help clean, polish, wash and bring order to the room. Toys that are torn or broken are either repaired or removed. We also care for our outdoor environment — the plants, trees, and animals we encounter during outside play. Children learn from these examples to care for each other by absorbing this kind of attitude. In such ways the children experience the soul warmth that Soesman described.

Cognitive Senses

The Sense of Hearing

The ear has three parts: the outer, middle, and inner ear. Our sense of hearing allows us to differentiate sounds such as a clanging spoon, a ringing bell, or a booming drum. Sounds make a deep impression on us. Children cannot block out harsh sounds around them. So again, it is best to protect them by leaving them at home if we are going to an excessively noisy place. Even as an adult, I have difficulty shopping in malls. The music in the halls and stores leaves me feeling confused and sometimes unable to make decisions. A child's sensitive ears magnify this effect. A parent may find relief from winter cabin fever at the shopping mall, but it is both an auditory and visual overload for her child.

Children are often exposed to electronic background sounds from such sources as car radios, CD players and television. These can be an onslaught to the sense of hearing. The children's attention is divided between the task at hand and the background music, weakening their ability to focus on their play.

In Waldorf kindergartens, we are aware of this noise sensitivity. We speak in soft voices and stimulate the children's sense of hearing with lyre music, singing, and storytelling. We want the quality of the sounds to be in harmony with the child's stage of development. In the complex interrelationship of sound experiences, the working of natural laws also works on the development of the child's own body. Of course, the whole morning is not spent hearing only soft tones; children can also be loud at times. But in our classrooms, the louder sounds are natural, not mechanical or electronic.

The Sense of Speech

The sense of speech allows us to be aware of the language another human being uses when she is communicating with us. The sense of speech allows us to grasp the way language works, how its words and sentences are formed, how meaning derives from their sounds and placement, and how we can use words to express our deepest thoughts and feelings. The next sense, the sense of thought, gives us the capacity to recognize what another person means to convey "beyond her words." In the process of this spoken communication, we take part in the genius of our spoken language. Through this sense, we come to perceive the world through the feelings that the sounds of our language evoke and we're placed firmly within the culture and society that uses our language. The sense of speech is thus a key factor in our social understanding. Steiner speaks at great length about the whole process connected with learning one's language and the way it shapes a human being at all levels.

There are qualities of sounds in language that communicate a great deal to human beings. The consonants are the structural element of language, its skeleton so to speak, while the vowels are more expressive. As we listen to each other, these sounds convey the experience of the entire culture that is home to the language we speak. Someone speaking Spanish will conceive of the human *I* through the feeling and tones of *yo*, while a German speaker will have a completely different conception because German uses the sounds of *ich* to name the human *I*.[4] Each language has unique qualities of its own that distinguish it from all other languages. Soesman uses the example of the Czech language. With its strong consonant sounds, Czech has quite a different effect on human beings than a language using more vowel sounds, such as French or Italian.

Full participation in the uniquely human event of spoken language requires person-to-person communication. The real genius of language and the sounding of words simply cannot be conveyed adequately through machine-to-person reproductions of human speech. We adults can, it is true, make do and compensate for the unreality of reproduced sound, but we can bring our whole life's experience to the task. A young child does not have such a capacity, and the limitations of recorded speech for a child's development of a healthy sense of speech

---

[4] For more information on this aspect of the sense of speech see Rudolf Steiner, *A Psychology of Body, Soul, and Spirit* (Hudson, NY: Anthroposophic Press, 1999), 31–32.

are, in my opinion, severe. Martin Large says this so very well in *Who's Bringing Them Up?*:[5]

> Children learn to speak through imitating, listening to and conversing with real, live people. They need to make contact with the genius of language, with its life, its sense and movement through other speakers. Mechanically reproduced voices on television are no substitute for real conversation. I hope the experiment will never be done, but I would venture the hypothesis that it would be impossible or very difficult for a young child to learn to speak through the television medium alone.
>
> As mentioned previously, television watching may blunt a commitment to language by delaying the development of the verbal areas of the brain at a crucially language-sensitive age.
>
> The importance of "Mum, speak to me," cannot be overemphasized. Babies first hear conversation around them, and probably understand a great deal when spoken with. In the later months, they exercise their vocal organs through babbling, and begin to imitate words, often repeating them over and over again. Television, as opposed to a brother, sister or parent, does not wait for a response, nor does it have a smiling face or a warm hug.
>
> Imitation, rehearsal, and repetition help the toddler master words, phrases and meanings from other people—conversation being the optimal condition for language

---

[5] Martin Large, *Who's Bringing Them Up?* (Stroud, England: Hawthorn Press, 1980), 72.

> development. Repeating rhymes like "Little Bo Peep" or "Pat-A-Cake Baker's Man" help with clarity of speech, with getting a real feel for the language, for discovering the excitement in words and rhythm. A child with a rich fund of nursery rhymes, songs and stories will have a head start at school.

In Waldorf schools, the artistic use of language is part of the curriculum. Stories and fairy tales are told using rich verbal imagery that reflects their classical tradition. Often the children have to stretch a bit in their understanding of certain words, but within the context of the story, new words become accessible to them. They become familiar with how language works in a story. At circle time it is similar. We use large and small gestures as we say nursery rhymes or poems or sing seasonal songs. This brings an artistic quality to language that speaks to the children in a living way. When the teacher conveys these verses and stories to children with honesty and vivid inner pictures, it heightens their sense of awareness and enhances their sense of speech.

The Sense of Another's Thought

Children live in a world surrounded by the thoughts of grown-ups long before they are able to understand those thoughts. As their sense of another's thought develops, they gradually gain the ability to understand, comprehend, and picture what those thoughts convey.

If you have ever traveled to another country, you may remember having a sense of what someone was trying to tell you, even though there was a language barrier between you. Each of you may have pantomimed, pointed, or even spoken to each other in your own respective language, and somehow been able to communicate. This is, perhaps, a close approximation of what it must be like for very young children to live surrounded by adult thoughts and speech.

Perhaps you have also had the experience of explaining something when your words suddenly became twisted, or you used an incorrect word in your sentence, but the other person understood the meaning anyway. Or someone may have tried to express something to you and couldn't find the appropriate words. Through your sensing of her thought, you may have helped her find the right word.

Through these experiences we become aware that we can picture the ideas behind someone else's words even when their words don't really express their ideas. We can enter the thought of another through this sense. This sense of thought connects us with each other beyond our words. It guides us to what lives within our fellow human beings as their ideas and concepts, and we are able to comprehend what they endeavor to express through words.

In our morning circle we weave a single thread of thought through the particular poems, nursery rhymes, and seasonal songs we have chosen, and express this cohesive meaning through gestures. With our stories it is similar. The teacher's inner thought pictures invite the children into the story she is telling, so that they follow this thread as it winds its way through the characters and actions of the story. Such activities nourish the sense of another's thought.

The Sense of Another's "I"

This sense is closely related to the sense of touch. At the beginning of a child's life we repeatedly cuddle, nurse, and speak to the child. Through these experiences, the infant has an inner communication with another human being. Touching and holding gradually help the child to become comfortable with other people. By developing this sense of who the other person is, a child becomes sensitive to someone else's individuality.

Young children experience the world long before their sense of another's individuality develops sufficiently to allow them to be fully aware of their perceptions. Who is the person standing behind the words or deeds? Is he warm-hearted, honest, and sincere? Or is he disinterested in the child, untruthful, self-seeking? Instinctively the child senses the reality behind the person. But the young child's own ego has not yet developed the strength to protect herself against these negative experiences. Her confidence and trust to unconsciously open up to meet the "I," or the individuality, of another person is undermined. This may have an adverse effect on the healthy development of the child's senses. Experiencing the other person's deceit makes the child believe that she can't trust her own sense of who the other person is. Her inner sense is telling her something different from what the person proclaims himself to be. Of course, all of this takes place at a level below the child's conscious awareness. Later as adults, we may discover that our early experiences have affected our ability or willingness to open up to other people.

Steiner pointed out that young children experience the character of the people around them so intensely that it is of utmost importance that those people have integrity. The message of who the teacher is speaks louder than anything the teacher says. I remember hearing Henry Barnes[6] say at a parent meeting many years ago that a teacher teaches out of what he or she can become. For our young children, it is most important that we teachers and parents continually work on our own development and thus serve as positive role models.

Summary

All twelve senses are interdependent and interrelated. We have separated and defined them only to better understand

[6] A teacher and administrator at the Rudolf Steiner School in New York City.

each sense. It is clear that there is much in our modern world that can compromise the healthy development of these senses. There are devices that push our children's motor coordination beyond developmental limits, food that is processed and artificially flavored, and electronic media that mimics human companionship. Fortunately, it is also true that we human beings still have the capacity to gift our children with what they need in order to develop into adults who can grasp the fullness of the world around them. We parents and teachers can go forward with confidence, knowing our children will emerge from our care with well-developed capacities that embrace all of life.

Questions from Parents

Parent: Can you elaborate on the sense of life? Is the sense of life involved in giving us information about a specific physical pain we may have?

Barbara: Yes, from a burn on a finger to an oncoming headache above the eyes. If you get up in the morning and feel unusually heavy in your body or if you feel unwell, your sense of life is giving you this information. But this sense also gives you the more general feeling of well-being.

Can you imagine how it would be for a child if his sense of life were not developed? Pain is a great educator. For example, after a number of falls on the stairs, a little child learns to hold on to the railing.

Parent: Does the sense of life have a psychological as well as a physical aspect to it? For example, if your child is going through a fearful period with night terrors, is this fear also connected to the sense of life?

Barbara: We never speak only about the physical aspect of the sense of life or of any of the senses, for that matter. And neither do we experience the senses in isolation. The senses work in conjunction, interweaving with each other. So, yes, the sense of life is also involved with psychological experiences. We know from our experience that a poor night's sleep, from whatever cause, may result in a weepy, cranky child the next day. He just feels out of sorts. But night terrors can come from many different sources and it is important to check with your pediatrician.

Parent: Mrs. Patterson is making a good point. Our society tends to put information into separate categories. As first-time parents, we are oriented to thinking about either the physical or psychological aspects of our child.

Barbara: It is worth reviewing what Steiner had to say about the nature of the human being. He said that the human being has a four-fold nature: a physical body we see and can touch; an etheric or life body that brings life to this material body and is the substance of our mental pictures; an astral or soul body that allows us to feel joy, sorrow, and desire and gives us the capacity of reason; and a spirit body that is the vehicle for what is unique in each of us, for what we call "I."

These aspects of our being interpenetrate and are dependent upon one another. What affects the astral body, affects the other bodies as well. What affects the physical body, affects the sense of life. To go back to your question — we can understand that the effect of a bad dream can bring about a disturbance in this sense of well-being.

Parent: Is there a way to cultivate a healthy sense of life in our children?

Barbara: Through healthy living. In not overtaxing their sense of life we help them to develop it. Consistent rhythms in the home, good food, not too many sweets, enough rest, proper clothing for the weather, staying out of noisy shopping centers, limiting media exposure; all the things we discussed earlier contribute to the healthy development of the senses. The senses will develop in a healthy way if they are not interfered with and are gently stimulated.

Parent: Don't you find that some children are able to express their needs at an earlier age, to say, "Mommy, I'm hungry," or "Mommy, I want to go to bed now." Other children don't have this awareness. They just know they can't stand the vague overall misery they are feeling, so they whine or fight with a sibling or protest about some simple request that would not normally bring such a reaction.

Parent: They all seem to have different relationships to food or sleep. I have a child who can skip lunch and still be fine after school. It often seems she has no need for food. On the other hand, my older child will be predictably out of sorts if she still has a full lunch box at three o'clock.

Barbara: There is no point trying to explain to your child that she will be fine as soon as she eats. Just get her some food, put it in front of her, and her mood will most likely change after eating.

Parents: Infants tell us when they are hungry. Why don't older children know they are hungry? What happens to the instinctive feeling of hunger that a little baby expresses through crying?

Barbara: These first cries come out of a strong instinctive nature. As the individuality of a child develops and his thinking capacity increases, these instinctive forces aren't as strong. As the child approaches two or three years of age and gets swept up in what is going on around him, he no longer reads his own signals as well as before. We parents do the reading for our child when he is small. We know the glassy eyes of an approaching fever or the whine of an overly tired baby. But as our children get a little older, we often don't read their signals as well as we used to, either.

Parent: Are there therapeutic ways to help your two- or three-year-old build up a healthy sense of balance if you have already interfered with this sense by using walkers and jump seats?

Barbara: Walking is a wonderful help in bringing the body into a right relationship with movement and balance. The climbing bars at the park also help, as well as games like hopscotch or jump rope.

Parent: My oldest child, who had a walker and a jump seat and loved them, has had the most difficult time with walking. She gets very tired and her knees are a little bit off. I often wonder how much these symptoms can be blamed on the jump seat. She was a very "outer space" child, and the jump seat made her feel like she was flying. Of course, at the time we didn't know there could be a problem later on with letting her do what she so enjoyed.

Parent: What about ballet or organized sports as a way of developing the sense of movement in your child? Some parents feel their child's desire for organized sports is so strong, even at the age of three, that they must allow their child to participate in that sport.

Barbara: These organized activities involve children in unnatural movements. Children don't naturally walk through the world on their toes, as in ballet, or use their legs and feet in the way an adult would in a soccer match. Organized sports develop muscles in ways that would not happen if a child moved about running, jumping, climbing, and walking as he would in normal play.

Creative Discipline

What is discipline? How does it fit into our view of the young child as an imitative being? As imitators, children cannot help doing what they see grown-ups doing. They unconsciously participate in the life around them, repeating adult words, mimicking adult actions, singing back songs adults sing to them. According to Rudolf Steiner, this imitation goes much deeper than just learning various behaviors; it affects children's digestive processes and the development and function of their inner organs.[1]

Imitation and Self-Discipline

A child at the imitative stage of development absorbs every aspect of his environment, which then becomes part of the innermost stirrings of his will, deep below the level of consciousness.

From birth onward, a young child is strongly affected by her parents and the other adults in her surroundings. What those adults do in a child's presence becomes part of her growth and development; if certain deeds are repeated regularly around the child, they become habit. Instinctively, the child will imitate these grown-ups. A child at this stage imitates everything in much the same way that adults imitate someone they see yawning.

This suggests to us that the most effective discipline for the young child has to do with the self-education of the adults around the child. Erich Gabert, in *Education and Adolescence*,[2] addresses teachers on this subject:

---

[1] Rudolf Steiner, *At the Gates of Spiritual Science*, Lecture 6, August 27, 1906 (London: Rudolf Steiner Press 1970), 51–60.

[2] Erich Gabert, *Education and Adolescence*, trans. Ruth Pusch (Hudson, NY: Anthroposophic Press, 1988), 30.

Children like to imitate adults

The growing and developing in the child listens to the growing and developing in the teacher. Therefore, just as much as the teacher works on himself, so much can he work on his pupils and so he can teach them. Education and self-education are one and the same. This knowledge takes away the sense of inadequacy. The question is not how far I have come and how much I can accomplish, but rather that I must constantly struggle. I can give to the children to the same degree that I work on myself.

In *The Kingdom of Childhood*,[3] Rudolf Steiner says that the child in the first seven years is really an eye. If someone has fits of temper and becomes furiously angry either with the child or in the presence of the child, the child will have the picture of this outburst throughout his entire being. As a result, this inner picture passes over into the processes of blood circulation, breathing, and metabolism, and, according to Steiner, the results remain in the child for the rest of his or her life. Everything we do in the presence of the child goes in deeply. Scolding, threats, and yelling do not help in disciplining young children. This approach may actually weaken their ability to deal with situations later in life. They get a little shock from these experiences. If these shocks occur regularly, children create barriers to protect themselves. Their souls harden a bit, and we find that we just can't seem to get through to them.

If we preach at a child, she does not really hear the message because she must erect a barrier against the anger we are emanating. This barrier prevents her from perceiving our message. What she will learn is to express anger, distance herself from others, and preach at those who displease her.

---

3 Rudolf Steiner, *The Kingdom of Childhood*, Lecture 2, August 13, 1924, trans. Helen Fox (Hudson, NY: Anthroposophic Press, 1995), 34.

Reforming the Space

When children in a Waldorf kindergarten misbehave, it usually means they have "fallen out of the form" of the moment. How can we recreate the form around them? I have found a number of things that work well. For example, if a child becomes too loud or too silly at snack time, I stand behind him and begin straightening the chair, fixing his place mat, cup, plate—in other words "re-forming" the space around him.

If this happens during playtime, I first check to make sure that none of the dolls or puppets are on the floor. A doll is an image of the human being for young children, and if a doll is on the floor where it can be inadvertently trampled or kicked aside, children see a chaotic picture of the human being. After I have checked on the dolls and puppets, I begin "re-forming" the main play areas: dusting and ordering shelves and picking up toys left behind in disorder. Then we begin to set a beautiful, orderly snack table. Many times such activities alone will restore harmony without the teacher speaking or doing anything directly with the children whose play has become chaotic. If a particular child is having difficulty, I make sure that her hair is tidy. I'll tuck in a shirt or retie a sash.

If we save our "no's" for situations where children are doing something dangerous or when they may damage someone's belongings, they will more readily listen to those "no's" when they are necessary. If we use the word "no" too often or indiscriminately, children soon learn to ignore it. If we just say "No," or "Don't do that," or "Stop that" for every situation, children stop in their play and look at what they are doing in a more self-conscious way. If, instead, we say what they may do with a toy, for example, we redirect their energy, and their play can go right on without interruption.

One day in my early childhood class, I was ironing our snack placemats during the children's playtime. Two little girls were playing with some knitted animals. They started tossing them in the air, so I got a woolen ball for them to play with. That distracted them momentarily, and they began tossing the ball. I went back to my ironing. Before long, they put the ball down and started tossing the animals again. I kept my attention on them while I completed the last of my work and put away the iron and ironing board.

Then, I got a large wooden barn down from the shelf and suggested that we make a home for the animals. The girls helped put the barn pieces together, and at my suggestion, they found some suitable bowls for food and water. They also brought some little stones and nuts to use for food. We continued expanding the scene with a blue cloth for a river and some felt fish. At this point, I withdrew from direct involvement with their play.

I had helped the girls create a positive form of play with the knitted animals, without ever saying, "Don't play with the animals like that." I had shown them what they *could* do with the animals. I also noticed that this situation and its resolution affected the children playing in the rest of the room, and their play became more harmonious.

Clear Messages and Limited Choices

Our communication with children needs to be clear. If we give directions to them in the form of a question, we create confusion. "How about hanging up your coat?" or "Can you get dressed now?" or "Would you put your shoes on?" implies they have a choice to do as we ask or not. When my son was about six years old, I experienced the results of such unclear questions. One day I said to him, "Wouldn't you like to clean up your room?" He became very upset with me and said, "If I say no, you will be angry with me."

I heard another type of confusing question at a school holiday fair some years ago. A mother was speaking to her little girl of about two. "Do you want to eat here or go home and eat?" The little girl did not answer, so the mother repeated the question, "Do you want to eat here or go home and eat?" Still the little girl did not answer. The child's father joined them, and the mother described the situation to him. The father took up the questioning where the mother had left off, "Do you want to eat here, or go home and eat?" The little girl began to cry. Then the mother said, "She's tired. Let's go home." The child obviously felt burdened at being asked to make decisions for the family.

Similarly, when we ask our young children what they want to eat, they experience something like we experience when we go to a restaurant that offers a large menu. The decision can be overwhelming, even for adults. When our children were growing up near Pittsburgh, Pennsylvania, we used to stop at the Howard Johnson restaurants when traveling on the Pennsylvania Turnpike. The children usually wanted ice cream, especially if the weather was warm. So I asked them what flavor they wanted. The advertising slogan for Howard Johnson's was that they offered twenty-eight flavors of ice cream. Our son, Paul, wanted to hear the names of all twenty-eight flavors of ice cream every time we went. The choices must have overwhelmed him: he always said, "I guess I'll take vanilla."

Asking our children what they want to wear or do creates a similar feeling within them. We are calling the "I want" aspect of their personalities out of them prematurely. They become more and more conscious of their likes and dislikes. "I want" then becomes part of their vocabulary when eating, getting dressed, going to bed, or accompanying mother to the store. Social problems emerge. We have all witnessed or been part of the supermarket scene: "I want" cookies, candy, or a particular cereal with a toy inside the box.

In the long run, offering children choices breeds egotism: they become self-centered and less sensitive to the needs of others. Offering choices to young children acts like a poison in their souls. As they grow older, they may not want to do the things life requires of them: school work, housework, or garden chores. Our battles with our teenagers are often a direct consequence of this kind of child-centered upbringing. No child is more insecure and dissatisfied than one who has been catered to in this way.

In a lecture for parents, Eugene Schwartz[4] humorously illustrates this dilemma of the myriad choices parents offer their children from the minute they get up in the morning.

Good morning, dear. What do you want to wear?

> A sleeveless jumper, a short-sleeved dress, or long-sleeve dress?
> Flared skirt, denim skirt, or flowered skirt?
> Short-shorts, capri pants, hiking shorts, or pants?

---

[4] An experienced Waldorf teacher, lecturer, author and now director of Waldorf Teacher Education at Sunbridge College, Chestnut Ridge, NY.

Pants and a shirt. Good. Which ones?

> Red, blue, green, striped, checked or plaid pants?
> Straight-legged, flared, roll-up, or regular-cut designer jeans?
> Tank top, turtleneck, short sleeved, or long-sleeved shirt?
> A shirt with a cartoon character, cereal box hero, or plain front?
> 100% cotton, cotton-polyester mix, cotton with lycra or spandex?

Let's have breakfast. What would you like to eat today?

> Orange, cranberry, grapefruit, or mango-tangerine-guava juice?
> Granola with nuts, honey, brown sugar, or with organic fruit?
> Served with 2%, 1%, soy-based milk, cream, or low-fat yogurt?
> Regular or cinnamon toast, English muffin, or bagel?

And the list grows longer. As parents in the audience recognize themselves, their laughter almost drowns out Eugene's voice before he is even halfway through his litany.

How did we get into this trap? Some of us were brought up with such strong authoritarian discipline that we'd rather not employ it with our own children. But the pendulum may have swung too far the other way, resulting in too little structure, too much confusion. Many children are suffering from too little discipline.

The Magic Word: May

There is a magic word, not authoritarian or permissive, which works well with children. The word is *may*. "You may hang up your coat." It contains no question to answer or ignore. In the word *may* is the quality of privilege. "You may place your boots on the mat."

I have also heard parents say to their children, "You may hang up your coat," but then weaken the statement by tacking on "OK?". Is this an effort to soften what seems too demanding a request? What does the "OK?" mean? If it isn't OK, does that mean the child doesn't have to do it? Does the child have a choice, or not? This can create confusion and insecurity for the child. The child feels most secure when he knows that his parents, teachers, and caregivers know what is best for him.

A mother of one of the girls in my kindergarten told me the following story. One late fall morning she was getting her two children off to school. There was the usual bustle of breakfast, packing lunches, and reminding the children that they needed to leave soon or they would be late for school. Since the temperature had dropped significantly during the night, the mother told her daughter that she would need to wear her snow pants. The girl protested and an argument began. Feeling the pressure of time, the mother gave in but took the snow pants along under her arm.

Shortly after the car pulled away from the house, the mother heard her daughter crying softly in the back seat and asked what was the matter. "I'm cold," said the little girl.

You can imagine what happened next.

"I told you it was cold outside, and that you needed to wear your snow pants," replied the mother. "You just wouldn't listen to me!"

The little girl remained silent and then said, "But you're my mother, and you should know what's best for me." Whereupon the mother drove her car to the side of the road and helped her daughter put on her snow pants.

Steiner expanded this point further by saying that no greater harm can be done to the child than giving directions as to what he must do and then reversing these directions.[5] He noted that children's resulting confusion from unclear adult thinking is the actual root of the so-called nervous diseases prevalent among adults in modern civilization. Steiner said this in 1923!

But what if our child throws a temper tantrum over something we have told him that he may or may not do? How can we respond so that we can best help our child? If we remain calm, quiet, and centered, our child absorbs this, and it brings him stability again. Our child absorbs our striving for self-discipline, and this restores harmony. If we try to explain too much to children, to reason with them about what we want them to do or not do, we prematurely awaken their capacities of reason

---

[5] Rudolf Steiner, *Education and Modern Spiritual Life*, Lecture 6, August 10, 1923 (Blauvelt, NY: Steinerbooks, 1989),105–119.

and intellect and pull them too early out of the dreamier world of childhood. Through imitation, they start trying to out-reason us and become extremely good at it. Rudolf Steiner said that it is possible to awaken a child's sense of what is right or wrong only toward his fifth year.

Rhythm

Earlier we spoke about the importance of rhythm and the role it plays in the lives of young children. It is also a great help with discipline. Like a heartbeat or the rising and setting of the sun, our classroom rhythms hold children in a secure balance. Our outer activity comes to meet whatever wells up within the children as we move through repetitive daily and weekly rhythms.

Healing Action

But practically, how do we deal with unacceptable behavior in a consequential way? How do we deal with children who hit, bite, scratch, kick or spit? If hands are hitting, we can wrap the hands in a silk cloth and let the child sit next to us until his or her hands get warm. "When your hands are warm and strong, they don't hit," we say to the child. With kicking feet, it is the same. A child who bites can be given a large piece of apple or carrot and must sit beside the teacher to eat it. "We bite the carrot, not our friends." For a child who scratches, bring out the healing basket and trim the child's nails. "Kittens scratch, but not children." A child who spits may be taken to the bathroom to spit into the toilet.

What do we do about the child who plays in a violent way? Oftentimes parents engage in roughhousing with this type of child, so that he will "get it out of his system." But children don't store violent play in a container that can be easily emptied. Real work is the cure for violent play: work in the garden, for example, digging holes, moving stones, carrying wood. Through such purposeful work, the child's chaotic will

gradually becomes more harmonious. Lots of physical exercise like swimming, long walks, and winter snow play also helps.

Consequent Action

Between the ages of two and four years, young children can be very stubborn. During this time, it is best if we overlook some of their negative reactions. Just go with your child and help him do what you want him to do, without anger or lots of explaining. Have confidence in his development. Don't waiver or allow him to wiggle around and out of what you have said needs to be done, or he will find your weak spot and "push your buttons" again and again.

If I have an older child in my class who is ready to enter first grade in the fall and is beginning to challenge the rules in a stronger way, I have sometimes found it is best to back off and give that child a little space. After I have clearly stated what she needs to do, I go on with my work, keeping my attention on her. If consistency over time has been my habit, and the child knows I will follow through, she will usually respond to me, especially if she feels my warmth and love surrounding her. This works better than a battle of words and wills.

Teachers and parents need to be good listeners. If a child is having difficulties with a classmate or sibling, it really helps if he can describe to you what is happening and feel that you are really listening to him with full attention. Then it is often enough to say, "You may tell Johnny that you don't like that."

I am reminded of an incident following an evening talk I once gave on the subject of discipline. There had been a good turn out, and parents seemed to appreciate my suggestions. We had a lively discussion about discipline, and I was pleased with how the evening had gone.

The very next morning two four-year-old girls in my class were playing together in the little house area. Suddenly, a loud argument erupted. I heard, "My father can build a better house than your father." This child's father happened to be an architect. The other girl began shouting about what her own father could do better. Then I heard, "I'm going to tell teacher!"

Both girls came running to the table where I was working with a six-year-old child. The two angry girls simultaneously began pouring out bits and pieces of the story and blaming each other for what had happened. I listened carefully, wondering what I could say or do to diffuse the fireworks. I had just given a talk on discipline the evening before! But at that moment no inspiration came to me. I felt paralyzed inside and knocked down a few pegs from the feeling I had had the evening before.

Then, in a perfectly calm voice the six-year-old standing next to me said, "Oh, just go start over." The two little girls looked at each other, said, "OK," turned around and walked back to the little house area and resumed their play. Apparently just being listened to allowed them to take in the simple solution from the six-year-old, and peace was restored.

We may have a situation where a child wants some river stones or dishes for house play and another "household" has taken more than its fair share of these items. Then, I suggest to the child that she get a bowl or a basket and go knock on her neighbor's "door" with the request to borrow some dishes or stones. This gives a form to the request that is harder to refuse and usually results in a positive response.

And what about "tattletales"? If this is more than an occasional problem, it can reveal a difficulty or social weakness in the tattler. How can we help this child? We involve him in our work, not as a punishment, but to feel the teacher's creative strength focused on a particular activity. If we are sewing, we find a pretty piece of material and let him create something, also. Washing dishes is a wonderful healer in such situations. Pouring warm, soapy water back and forth in the little baby food jars we use for painting is great fun and helps smooth over momentary irritations. Baking is also a wonderful healer. The bakers bring their combined efforts into measuring, stirring, and kneading the dough for the benefit of the whole class.

Positivity

Sometimes a child just needs to be held in the rocking chair for a while or, if obviously tired, we make him a bed on the sofa with a pillow and some cotton cloths for blankets. A flock of "nurses" usually gathers around to care for such a child, who then becomes woven back into a play situation again. Criticizing, scolding, or belittling children does not help. If we do this regularly, a child may either turn us off in a seemingly passive way or become more aggressive. It's always better to work with positive, encouraging words that help a child feel good about himself.

Guidance

The greatest help with discipline comes from the spiritual work the teacher undertakes. This is part of the self-education I mentioned earlier. Over the years, I have experienced that if I carry each child's difficulties with me into my sleep life, asking the angel of the child for help, then often just the right thoughts, the right words, the right actions come to me the next day when working with that child. Then I am able to offer the kind of correction that gives children the opportunity to develop and unfold their best possibilities.

Conclusion

In closing, I would like to describe a situation that occurred between a mother and her two children who were in my parent-child class. The older child was a willful and energetic three-year-old. His younger brother was about six months old. During class discussions with the parents, discipline was an ever-recurring topic, and as teacher and parents we talked about how to work with these often very challenging emerging two- and three-year-old wills. As a result of these discussions, I offered a parent evening. The topic was "Guiding the Will of the Child from Birth to Seven Years."

Shortly after we began the meeting, the mother of the two previously mentioned boys recounted what had happened to her that day. That afternoon she had taken the children to the public library for an outing. Soon after they arrived, the three-year-old began wildly running up and down the aisles, disturbing everything and everybody.

What was this mother to do? She had her baby in a stroller so she wasn't free to run after the older child. He was oblivious as she called to him. She made the decision to park the stroller and baby off to the side and run after the three-year-old. He thought this was a great game and just kept running. When she finally overtook him and picked him up, he protested loudly while squirming and wiggling to get free, and by the time she returned to her baby, several adults had gathered around the stroller. They wondered if the baby had been abandoned and were talking about calling the police.

By now the mother was in a state of high agitation. Her three-year-old, who was still in her arms, continued to flail about, and the circle of people who had been drawn to the scene by the noise and excitement had grown larger. She announced that she was the baby's mother, and he had certainly not been abandoned. She then left the library as quickly as possible, returned home, and called her husband at work to pour out her frustrations. She told him he had to come home right then and take over the children. She was at the end of her rope.

Her husband gently reminded her that in a few hours she was going to attend the parent evening at school. He recommended that she hang on a little while longer.

As she told this story at the meeting that evening, we all surrounded her with our support and understanding. All parents have been in a situation like this where their nerves are frayed, their energy is depleted, and they feel inadequate to meet the challenges of parenting. Through sharing such challenges, teacher and parents feel supported by one another and can gain insights from each others' experience. But we should remember not to be too hard on ourselves. Children benefit also from our striving.

I believe that true discipline consists of guiding our young children out of imitation through self-discipline. We do this by creating and maintaining appropriate play spaces that nurture their imaginations, by communicating through clear messages with limited choices, by establishing consistent rhythms each day, by using real work to process anger, and by building our children's self-esteem through positivity.

Questions from Parents

Parent: All you've said makes so much sense. But as a parent of several small children, I find it hard to find time to step back and see how I can make changes at home that would lessen unpleasant or unhappy situations with our children. I am still in the trenches of parenting!

Barbara: All parents have hard days at home with their children. It is helpful to look back on the day's events after the children are in bed. You can ask yourself, "What led up to that explosion?" In a reflective way, ask yourself what you can learn from this situation. How could you be a few steps ahead next time to prevent this situation from happening? It won't help with today, that is over. But similar situations will come up again because children tend to present the same categories of challenges to us over and over again. They see our weaknesses and know how to "push our buttons." It helps so much to reflect on our particular challenges in order to improve the situation next time.

Parent: We have three small children. We have such a hard time sitting down at the table to eat together. It isn't pleasant at all.

Barbara: This will pass. You are not going to be able to maintain a peaceful atmosphere throughout your evening meals with children so young. But hold on to the ideal of what you are working towards. Do set the table nicely with flowers and placemats. Maybe you can maintain a peaceful atmosphere for only a few minutes but it is a start. You have to have confidence in the small changes for now. It is really enough.

Parent: I tried using the word "may" with my daughter after I attended one of your previous lectures. It worked so well! "You may clean that up now," I told her. It was much better than saying, "How could you do this to me? I just cleaned that floor!" She did as I asked her. It was great.

Parent: Can children accept yelling as "just the way Mom is," or is yelling always damaging regardless of the culture or habits of the family?

Barbara: I believe that yelling is always harmful to any child. When there is yelling in the home, the child hardens his soul in order to protect himself. He shields himself in order not to let the yelling in so deeply. Then, we as parents and teachers feel we can't get through to him when we are telling him something.

Parent: What do you do with a child who is restless and cannot engage himself in play at the moment? What do you do with a very active boy who is simply bouncing off walls on any given day?

Barbara: It becomes your challenge to incorporate the child into your own work. Real work is very important for children. They know the difference between busy work and real work.

If you can include the child in tasks such as in dishwashing or cutting up fruits and vegetables for dinner, this will give him time to regroup and imitate your positive work. This imitation is then available to him as he returns to his play activities by himself or with others. Real work can take a chaotic will and bring order to it.

When I ran a preschool in my home we had an old tree in our backyard that needed to be removed. The children were delighted when they were able to

Stomping the earth around the tree stump is satisfying work

assist my husband with that job. Once things were at a stage where it was safe for them to help, they were completely absorbed in filling little buckets with dirt and dumping them into the huge hole my husband had dug for burying the weighty roots left behind after the tree was cut down. Then the "stompers" went all around the edges, stomping down the soil. They had great fun doing this work.

Occasional wheelbarrow rides were also lots of fun both for my husband and for the children. Their clothes were usually quite soiled after this work but no parent ever complained. This tree removal became the topic of many dinner table conversations in the homes of the preschoolers and was such satisfying work for the children.

I introduced them to lots of woodcutter songs and verses in the morning circle each day, which brought an artistic quality to the work. It seemed to me at the time that every kindergarten should take down a tree or do a similar garden task.

Wheelbarrow rides are fun, too

Parent: Do children need more discipline today? It seems as if today's children are not held by rules of acceptable behavior as they once were. Could it be a result of the kind of lives we lead?

Barbara: I do believe the challenges our children present today are greater than those of previous generations. The world was smaller when I was growing up. The traditions of family life, community, and country had a stronger influence on children's and young peoples' behavior. My mother didn't drive. We weren't driven anywhere during the day when my father was at work. If we wanted to go somewhere, we walked. Our family had no TV. If we needed entertainment, we had to make our own fun.

But we are unable to roll back time. Most of us wouldn't even want to. Our concern is for our children who are growing up in a rapidly changing world where modern technology can take away their childhood. The influences of television and movies, highly sophisticated advertising techniques, and more worldwide travel have enlarged our children's world, bringing them more experiences outside the home where we have increasingly less control.

Even if our children don't watch TV or use computers, they may play with other children who do.

They may also experience their friends reacting to their own parents in aggressive or even dishonest ways, and decide to try that out at home. There are no easy answers but consistency of discipline and a healthy family life do help. I believe each child and adult has a guardian angel who protects and guides us in meeting what our destiny brings. As we trust in this help, we bring spiritual strength to our parenting and our children feel this strength.

Parent: How can I build self-discipline in my children when it is lacking in my own life since childhood? I don't have the self-discipline I need to be a good role model for them.

Barbara: It is never too late to begin working on self-discipline. Life presents us with a multitude of opportunities, and our children benefit from these efforts as well.

Parent: In so many contemporary publications, we read about empowering our children by giving them choices. How would you suggest we undo some of this empowerment we may have been fostering all along?

Barbara: You may have to start by defining the choice, for example, between the red and the blue outfit, especially if the child is used to a full range of choices. Offering children open-ended choices eventually leads to self-centeredness. Their likes and dislikes, what they want or don't want, become the focus of attention and lead to egotism. If adults are always asking them what they want to eat, or wear, or do, the children become more focused on themselves and don't so readily show interest in the needs of others.

Parent: How can we talk to our children in ways that are encouraging to them and not just critical?

Barbara: Discipline should never be an outlet for our anger, but a way of guiding our children into self-discipline as they mature. We must always work with the positive aspects of the children. We want them to grow up to be, as Rudolf Steiner said, "free human beings, able of themselves to impart purpose and direction to their lives."

Parent-Child Classes with Barbara

For the last three years I have been teaching parent-child classes at Great Oaks School, in Evanston, Illinois. These classes are for children ages 2½ to 4 years and meet for two hours once a week. The setting is similar to an early childhood, or kindergarten class, where children age 3–6 attend without their parents.

For some of the parents, this is their first experience of Waldorf education. The program provides opportunities to ask questions and learn more about the pedagogy through observing the teachers working with the rhythmic ordering of the morning and guiding the children in artistic activities such as coloring, watercolor painting, and beeswax modeling. The children also participate in the practical tasks of bread making, table setting, dish washing and cleaning up at the end of the session. Human relationships are enriched as parents, teachers and children bond while engaging in these simple activities with joy and enthusiasm.

A typical morning begins at 9:30. By 9:45, we begin our morning circle time. A little story unfolds through seasonal songs, nursery rhymes, and verses brought to life by movements that engage our bodies from head to toe. New words become accessible in the context of the poem or rhyme, and thus language skills are enhanced. Following the morning circle, there is a period of free playtime. Dolls are fed; houses are built of wooden play stands, cotton cloth and large clothespins; scenes are created on the floor using wooden or knitted animals together with pieces of irregularly shaped wood or cloth. Our rather undefined toys leave lots of room for stimulating the child's imagination.

A wooden tree house and a castle stimulate interactive play among the children. They begin to develop social skills like learning to share or having to wait for a toy someone else is playing with. This can be hard at this age, and sometimes teachers need to help. Parents then experience how teachers resolve such discipline issues.

Meanwhile the parents settle into their work—learning how to make Waldorf toys, doing simple crafts, and preparing the morning snack, all in sight of their children. Soft conversation among the parents creates a happy mood in the room. We know that young children learn primarily through imitation, so they are absorbing this mood in the room as well as the gestures and concentration of the adults on their tasks. This inspires the children for their work which we call play.

One of the artistic or practical tasks mentioned earlier may also take place during playtime. Some children want to help while other children may continue playing. At 10:30 parents put their handwork away, and prepare a lovely snack table. Everybody washes hands, and we all sit down at the table. We acknowledge the Earth and Sun with gratitude for our food, and all hold hands as we say, "Blessings on our snack."

After snack, some children return to their play while others help my assistant wash up the snack dishes. This allows me a fifteen- to twenty-minute discussion period with the parents on a chosen theme . The theme arises out of a book we are slowly working through, a handout I may have passed out the previous week, or a question someone may have. Then we sing our clean up song and all help put the toys away. We close the morning with a puppet show and good-bye verse and song.

We have at least one parent evening without children per ten week session where we have the luxury of uninterrupted conversation.

Parents say that the program enriches their family life. They get ideas about celebrating festivals at home and gain skills in ways to include their children in their day to day tasks of living. New friendships are formed which often last for years. Parents feel respected and supported in their important task. Through receiving the weekly school newsletter and being invited to participate in whole school festivals and fund raising events, the first links to the greater school community begin to be built.

Morning Schedule

Tuesdays and Wednesdays 9:30 A.M. – 11:30 A.M.

Rhythm of the Day

9:30 A.M. arrival time and settling in
9:45 A.M. morning circle
10:00 A.M. creative play for children

Activities for parents might include snack preparation, crafts and work projects as well as periodically baking and painting with the children.

10:30 A.M. snack and conversation
11:00 A.M. cleanup
11:15 A.M. puppet show
11:30 A.M. goodbye circle

Work Projects

mending cloths
sanding
repairing toys
washing placemats
sweeping, dusting, polishing tables, and ironing

Sample Songs and Verses[1]

Hand Washing

Song: Wash hands, wash, and dry them on the towel,
Soon its time to eat our snack so wash your hands now.

Snack Blessing

Verse: Earth who gives to us this food
Sun who makes it ripe and good
Dear Sun, dear Earth by you we live
And loving thanks to you we give.[2]

Goodbye Circle

Song: Hark children sweet music
Like of angels that sing
Flying high and flying low
Making silver bells ring

Verse: Heavens above and earth below
And angels flying to and fro
And on the earth so firmly I stand
I stretch out my hand — and say
Goodbye friends until we meet again

---

[1] Most Waldorf teachers know an extensive number of songs and verses to use with the children. Since many are passed from teacher to teacher, the original sources are frequently unknown.

[2] *Earth Who Gives to Us This Food* by Christian Morgenstern

Other Songs

Here We Go 'Round the Mulberry Bush

Chorus: Here we go 'round the mulberry bush,
The mulberry bush,the mulberry bush.
Here we go 'round the mulberry bush,
So early in the morning.

Verses: This is the way we wash our cloths...
This is the way we sweep our rooms...
This is the way we scrub our floors...
This is the way we wash our face...
This is the way we comb our hair...
This is the way we tie our shoes...
This is the way we go to school, etc.

I Can Reach So High

I can reach so high, I can touch the sky.
I can reach so low, I can touch my toe.
I can turn myself around and around.
And sit down quietly on the ground.

Rainbow Bridge Birthday Stories

Birthday Story for a Mixed-Age Kindergarten

As told by Barbara Patterson

Once upon a time in a land far yet near there lived a heavenly child. He worked in the house of the moon. He worked in the houses of the stars and he worked for a long time in the house of the sun. When he finished his work in each house, he received a gift.

One time, he was with his special friends when all of a sudden the clouds parted and he saw a beautiful, round jewel below. But just when he wanted to see more, the clouds came together again. He told this to one of the Angels that he felt especially close to. "You have seen the earth," said the Angel. "May I go down there?" asked the child. "Yes, you may go but it is not yet the right time," replied the Angel, and so the heavenly child went on with his friends and with his work in heaven.

Some time later the clouds again parted but this time the heavenly child saw all the rainbow colors on the earth. He saw the butterflies visiting the flowers and the birds flying in the air. They were beckoning to him as if to say, "Come here where we are." He saw the fish swimming in the river and the many different kinds of stones and plants that covered the earth. And he saw earthly children climbing trees, running and jumping in the meadows and walking through the crunchy leaves. It was all so beautiful!

He saw earthly fathers and mothers doing their work. One was a farmer, another a builder; and still others were bakers, shoemakers and shopkeepers. And he saw mothers and fathers caring for their children. Then he saw a woman and a man full of love and goodness. "Oh, I want to go to them," he said. But when he told his Angel, He said, "It is still not the right time. First you must go through the lands of dream."

And so the heavenly child went on a long journey through the lands of dream. There he had a wonderful dream about this special woman and man and he loved them very much. And in the dream he said, "I want to be in your family." The woman smiled with such a warm and welcoming smile and the man nodded his head and answered from his heart, "Yes." When the heavenly child told his Angel about the dream, the Angel said, "Now you are ready and I will accompany you on your journey." The gifts that you have received from the sun, the stars and the moon will help you with the work you have chosen to do on the earth."

And so together they traveled over the rainbow bridge and down the spiral staircase until they came to a big gate. The heavenly child felt a little anxious about leaving his wonderful heavenly home, but with courage in his heart and his Angel beside him, he went through the gate and . . . [pause] a little baby was born upon the earth. He opened his eyes and saw the woman and man from his dream. "Our little baby" they said. "We shall name him__________".

And so children, ___ years ago today, ___________ was born upon the earth. When he has finished his tasks here on earth, he will have a gift to take back to the moon and to the stars and to the sun.

Blessings on the Angel who led you to earth,
loving your dear Mother who gave you birth.[3]

[3] Source unknown

Barbara's Commentary on Birthday Stories

Telling a birthday story is a lovely tradition to begin when a child is very young. It can be created by a teacher, parent, friend — anyone special to the child. It is best told from memory rather than from reading a written version. To personalize the story for each child you can add some descriptive words just after the heavenly child first sees the woman and man full of love and goodness: for example — "who didn't yet have any children" or "who already had a little girl named Jane." The moment in my story when the child asks to be a member of the family is very special. To me it is like the moment of conception.

The references to the professions such as baker, shoemaker, and shopkeeper on the earth can have several meanings. In the first seven years the child is shaping and building his body to fit his growing individuality. The baker and shoemaker are the role models or images for this forming work and the shopkeeper (retail merchant) indicates readiness to meet the world that is coming to him. These professions give the child a glimpse into the future. We tell about these and others in our circle games and stories so that the children have a relationship to them.

The parents in my early childhood class usually provide the birthday snack and as we sit around the table, they share baby pictures and even describe some events from the child's first years. This sharing gives the parents a role in this class celebration which they appreciate very much.

Adoption Birthday Story

As told by Nancy Parsons

Were I still working in a kindergarten, this is a birthday story I would tell a young adopted child about her origins in Asia.

One day, about 3 years ago (use child's age), ______ and her Angels were looking down upon the earth, searching for just the right family to be her new parents. They looked high and low, they looked North, they looked South, but they just couldn't find a mother and father who could give _______ "everything" she needed.

They kept looking, for they were very determined. They looked up, they looked down, they looked East, they looked West. And when they looked East and West, they discovered something very special. In the East, they discovered a mother and a father who could give ________ the gift she would need first — they could open the door at the end of the rainbow bridge and place her, filled with life and joy, upon the Earth. But that was all they could give, and _______ and her angels knew she would need more.

Then, _______ and her Angels looked to the West, and they discovered something very special. They discovered a mother and a father who could not open the rainbow door or fill _______ with that first life, but they could give her a loving home where she could grow in joy and learn all she needed to know to love the Earth. ________ and her Angels looked at each other and smiled in deep happiness. They agreed that it should be done!

And so, on this day, 3 years ago, _______ slid down the rainbow bridge where her mother and father of the East waited to open the door to give her life and joy. And then, a few (days, weeks, etc.) later, with the help of many people and, of course, Angels, she came to her mother and father of the West, Mr. & Mrs. ________, and they opened their arms to carry her to her home of love and joy and life! Happy birthday, _______.

Birthday Story for a Kindergarten Child

As told by Nancy Foster

Once upon a time there was a little child who was still with the Angels in heaven, and he/she was very happy there. He looked at the beautiful colors and listened to the lovely music, and that was where he belonged. But one day it seemed to that child as if he had seen all that there was to be seen in heaven. So he looked out through the golden clouds, and there in the distance he saw the earth and suddenly he was filled with a great longing to go there.

And so he said to his Angel, "Please, may I go down to earth now?" but his Angel looked at him and said, "No, it is still too soon; you must wait a little while yet." So the child waited, and soon forgot about the earth, and was happy where he was.

Then one day he again longed to go down to earth, and so he said to his Angel, "Please, now may I go down to earth?" But his Angel looked at him and said, "No, it is still too soon; you must wait a little while yet." So the child waited.

Then one night as he slept, he dreamed a wonderful dream. He was walking about on earth among many, many people, and there he met a woman, and he loved her very much, and he said, "Will you be my mother?" And the woman said "Yes." Then he met a man and he loved him very much, and he said, "Will you be my father?" and the man said "Yes." So the child chose his parents in that beautiful dream.

As soon as he awakened, he told his Angel about his dream, and the Angel looked at him and said, "Yes. Now it is time for you to go down to earth. Your parents are waiting for you. But you must go alone; I cannot go with you. I will stay here and watch over you until you are ready to come back again."

"But how can I go alone?" asked the child. "You shall see," said the Angel. So the child went to dreamland, and while ten moons waxed and waned, he rocked in a little boat. And at the end of that time a beautiful colored rainbow stretched from heaven to earth, and on it the child came down to earth as a tiny baby, and his name was _______.

Events from each year of the child's life are added here. The following are examples of descriptions I have used:

> And his mother and father loved him very much and took good care of him, and he began to grow. And he learned to laugh and to sit up by himself and then he was ONE year old.
>
> And his grandma and grandpa came to visit from California and then he was TWO years old.
>
> And he liked to go on walks with his mommy and daddy and baby sister and visit the neighbor's dog and then he was THREE years old.
>
> And he went to the ocean for the first time and now he is FOUR years old.

Fairy Tales and Stories for Different Ages

Compiled by Joan Almon

When selecting fairy tales for young children, it is a help to know which tales tend to be appropriate for different ages. These are to be taken as light indications, not hard and fast rules. Reading a few tales from each category gives a picture of the progression of difficulty of the tales. One can then choose according to the needs and maturity of the child(ren) involved.

Very simplest tales and sequential tales; suitable for three and young four-year-olds:

Sweet Porridge (Grimm #103)
Silverhair (Goldilocks) and the Three Bears (Spindrift)
Little Louse and Little Flea (Spindrift)
The Giant Turnip (Russian, *Autumn Book)*
The Mitten (Russian)
The Gingerbread Man
The Johnny Cake (English)
*The Hungry Cat (Plays for Puppets)**
The Little House (Spindrift)
The Old Woman and Her Pig (English Fairy Tales)
The Cat and the Mouse (English Fairy Tales)
*The Little Boy Who Wanted to be Carried Along (Plays for Puppets)**
When the Root Children Wake Up
Little Red Hen
The City Mouse and the Country Mouse

Simple tales but slightly more complex than those listed above. The mood is usually cheerful and without too much sorrow and struggle. Quite good for four- and young five-year-olds:

The Three Billy Goats Gruff (Spindrift)
The Three Little Pigs
The Wolf and the Seven Little Kids (Grimm #5)
The Pancake Mill (Let Us Form a Ring)$^{\Delta}$
Mashenka and the Bear (Spindrift)
The Elves (Grimm #39)
Star Money (Grimm #153)
Huggin and the Turnip (The Seven Year Old Wonder Book)

In the next category many of the tales are associated with the term "fairy tale ." There is more challenge and detail than in the above list, obstacles are encountered but they do not weigh too heavily on the soul of the child. Good for five- and young six-year-olds.

The Frog Prince (Grimm #1)
Mother Holle (Grimm #24)
Little Red Cap (Grimm #26)
The Bremen Town Musicians (Grimm #27)
The Golden Goose (Grimm #64)
The Spindle, The Shuttle and the Needle (Grimm #188)
The Hut in the Forest (Grimm #169)
The Queen Bee (Grimm #62)
*The Snow Maiden (Plays for Puppets)**
The Seven Ravens (Grimm #25)
Snow White and Rose Red (Grimm #161)
Little Briar Rose (Grimm #50)

The Princess in the Flaming Castle (Let Us Form a Ring)$^{\Delta}$
Twiggy (Let Us Form a Ring)$^{\Delta}$
The Donkey (Grimm #144)
Lazy Jack (English Fairy Tales)
Tom-Tit-Tot (English Fairy Tales)
Rumpilstiltskin (Grimm #55)

The last category are those tales which are much loved by children but in most cases are better told in the first grade rather than in the kindergarten or early childhood classes. The challenges are more difficult in them and the force of evil more strongly described. Some kindergarten teachers may tell one or two of these tales at the end of the year if they have a number of children turning seven.

Little Snow White (Grimm #53)
Jorinda and Joringel (Grimm #69)
Hansel and Gretel (Grimm #15)
Cinderella (Grimm #21)
Rapunzel (Grimm #12)

Fairy Tale Resources:

Hunt, Margaret and James Stern, editors:*The Complete Grimm's Fairy Tales*
Introduction by Padraic Colum and commentary by Joseph Campbell.

Jacobs, Joseph, Editor: *English Fairy Tales*
Illustrated by John D. Batten

Wyatt, Isabel: *Seven Year Old Wonder Book*

Spindrift and *Autumn* books
Available through Rudolf Steiner College Bookstore, 9200 Fair Oaks Blvd., Fair Oaks, CA 95628.

* *A Lifetime of Joy* (formerly *Plays for Puppets*) compiled and created by Bronja Zahlingen.

† *Let Us Form a Ring* (formerly the *Acorn Hill Anthology*)

An enlarged and revised edition available through Waldorf Early Childhood Association of North America (WECAN), 285 Hungry Hollow Road, Spring Valley, NY 10977.

Interpretations of Fairy Tales

Glas, Norbert: *Once Upon a Fairy Tale*
Two volumes. Fascinating look at the "real meaning" of fairy tales.

Meyer, Rudolf: *The Wisdom of Fairy Tales*
The meaning of fairy tales and how they can have a positive influence on the developing child.

Steiner, Rudolf: *The Poetry and Meaning of Fairy Tales*
Contains 2 lectures given in 1908 and 1913 in Berlin.

Wilkinson, Roy: *The Interpretation of Fairy Tales*
Summaries and commentaries of fairy tales and their effects on the healthy soul life.

Handwork Instructions[4]

Simple Knot Doll

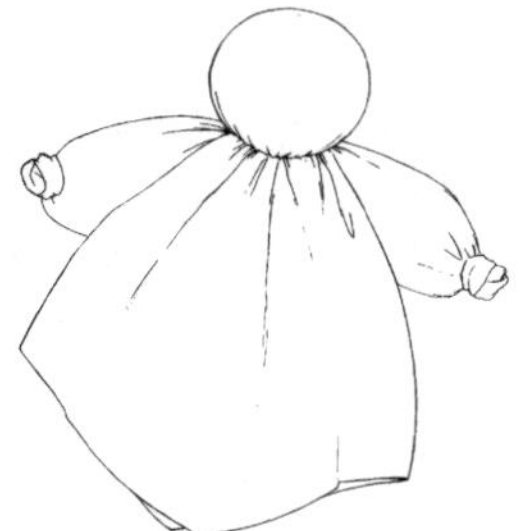

Materials

- 100% cotton flannel material (plain pastel shades)
- wool batting
- thread to match fabric
- strong thread (quilting or buttonhole thread works well) or you can use dental floss.

Head

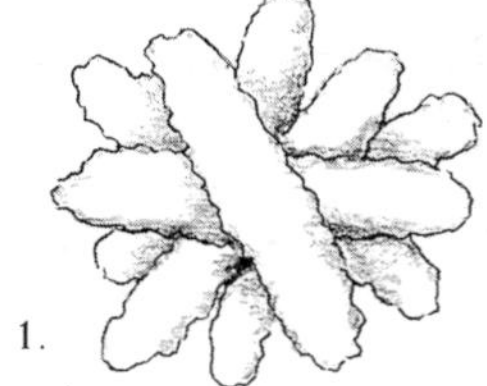
1.

1. To make the head, lay strips of wool batting on top of one another as shown in the diagram. You will need quite a lot of it.

2. Gather up the pile of the wool forming a fairly firm, nice round ball for the head. The head should be about 2½″ in diameter.

   If your head isn't quite large enough or smooth enough, you can add additional top layers at this point.

   If the neck has become too thick, you can "thin" it a little by pulling out some of the wool from the center.

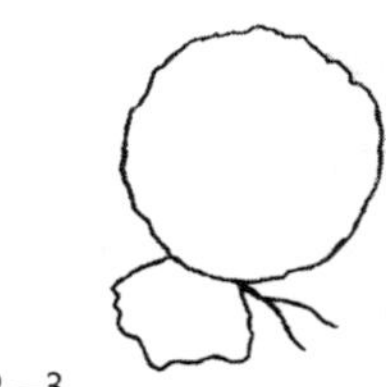
2.–3.

[4] NOTE: Adults should always be supervising babies and young children when they are playing with soft dolls and toys.

3. Now tie off around the neck with your strong thread or dental floss pulling it tightly and knotting securely.

Body

4. To form the body, cut a 3″ x 7″ rectangle from the flannel material. Fold the longer side in half and with right sides together, sew up a little sack, as illustrated. This measurement includes ½″ seam allowance along the sides and top of the sack. The top of the sack can just be turned under.

   Turn the sack right side out. This sack encloses the "tails" of the wool batting from the head and gives the body some weight. Some added wool batting may be needed to fill out the sack.

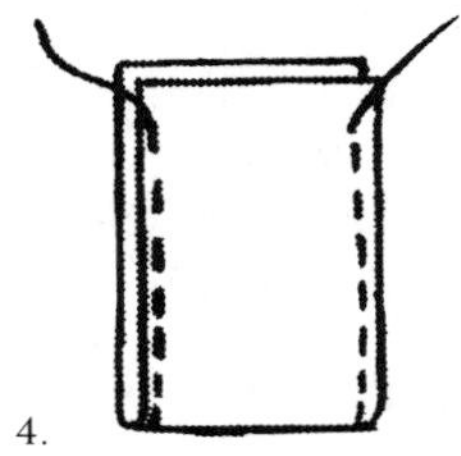

4.

5. Place the head inside this tube and sew a running stitch to attach the neck securely to the sack body. Some adjusting needs to be done at this point so the neck isn't too thick.

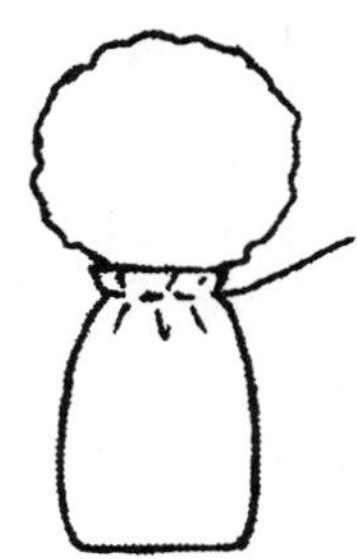

5.

6. Hem all four edges of a 20″ x 20″ square of flannel material. Find the center and mark with pins.

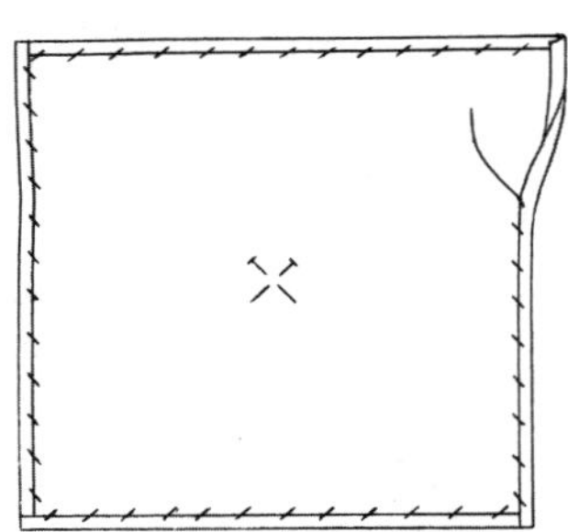

6.

7. Turn the hemmed square so the wrong side is facing you.

   Place the head and sack on top of the flannel matching the center point with the center of the top of the head. Be sure to line up the center of the face with the bottom point of the triangle.

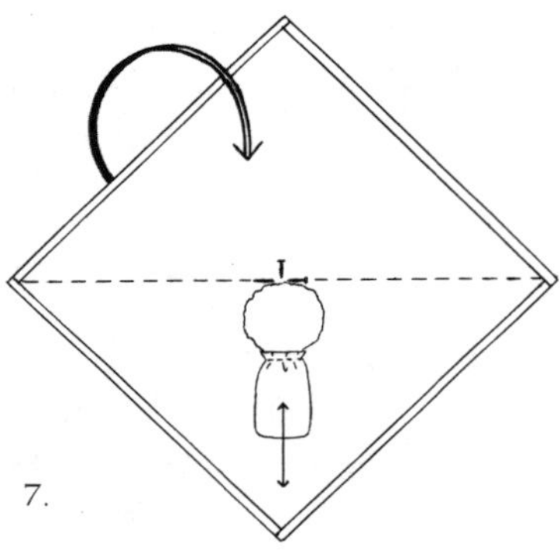

7.

   Gather the flannel material around the head smoothing the wrinkles from the side that will be the face.

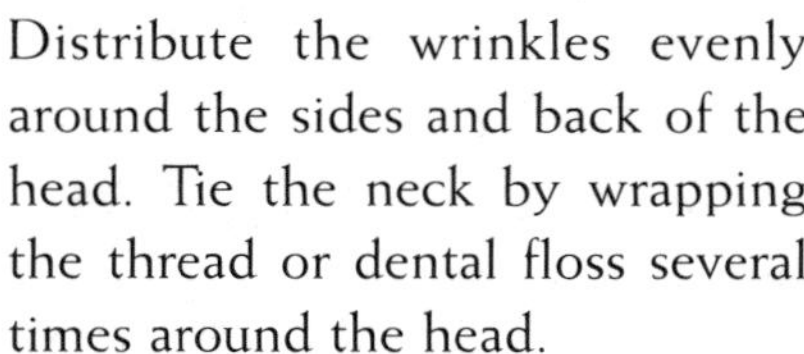

   Distribute the wrinkles evenly around the sides and back of the head. Tie the neck by wrapping the thread or dental floss several times around the head.

8. Knot the opposite ends of the triangle for hands and secure the knots with a few stitches.

Knot Doll With Arms and Legs and Matching Bonnet

Materials

- 100% cotton flannel — plain pastel shade
- matching ribbon and thread
- wool batting
- strong thread (quilting or buttonhole thread works well or dental floss)

Head

Follow the instructions for the Simple Knot Doll head # 1 – 3.

Body

4. Cut out the piece of flannel according to the dimensions in the diagram.

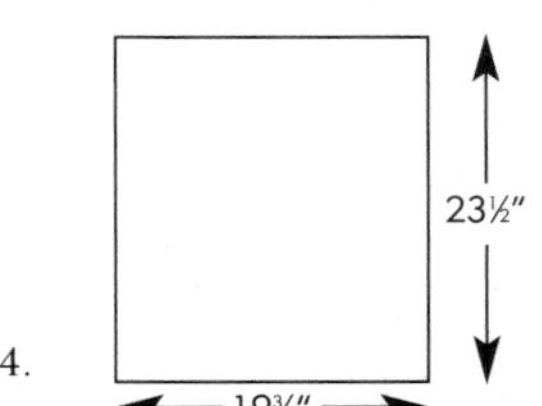

5. Fold over 7¾" and mark the center.

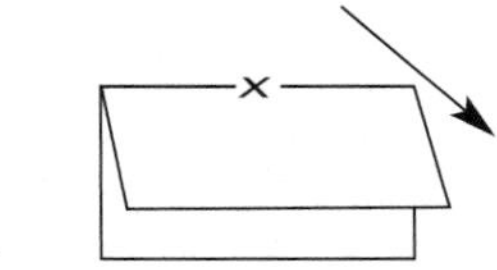

6. Place the head under the flannel matching the center point of the folded down piece of flannel with the center point at the top of the head.

   Gather the flannel around the head smoothing the wrinkles from the side that will be the face. Place this smoothed side of the head to the front. The short folded down piece of flannel will be the back of the doll. Tie around the neck with strong thread or dental floss pulling it tightly and knot securely.

   Mark the center of both ends of the flannel, as shown.

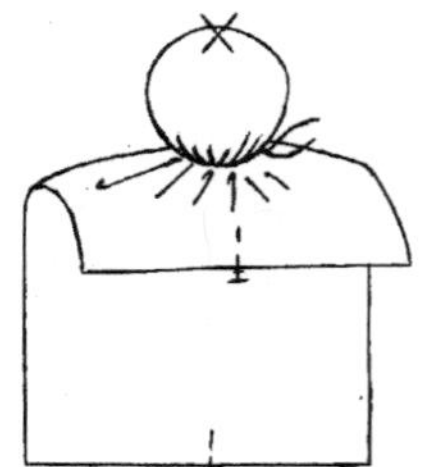

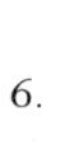

6.

Legs

7. To form the legs, turn the doll over so that the front side is facing you and sew up the legs, meeting at the center. The completion of this step is shown in illustration 8a.

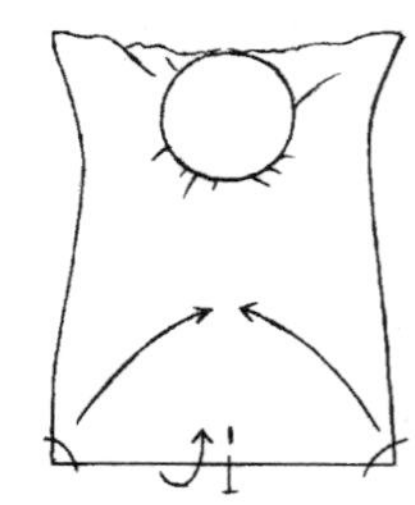

7.

Arms

8a. To form the arms, tuck the head under and bring the back flap over.

8b. Sew as shown, meeting at the center mark. Make sure that the opening is large enough to pull the head through it.

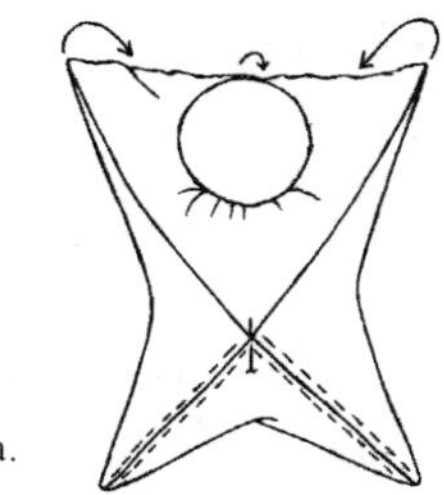
8a.

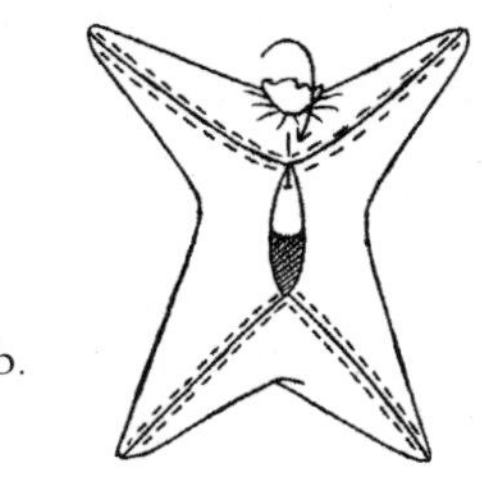
8b.

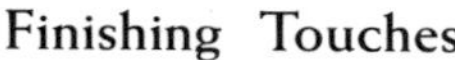

Finishing Touches

9. Pull the head through the opening turning the whole doll right side out. Fill the doll with wool batting so it is nice and plump but not packed. Stitch up the opening.

   Most dolls need to have the top piece of flannel that forms the arms pulled down and tacked. This brings the arms down so they are in a nice proportion with the the rest of the doll. Do this after the opening has been sewn shut.

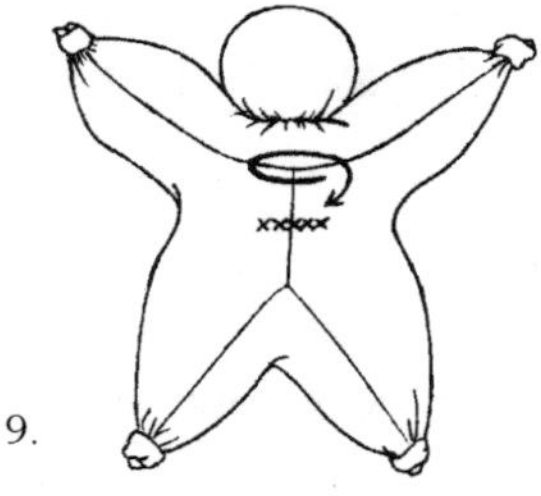
9.

Hands and Feet

10. To form the hands and feet, make little knots and tack in place with a few stitches.

Doll Bonnet

1. Measure the head, as shown, and cut a piece of flannel approximately 9½" x 4½"or your measurement plus 1". Seam allowance of about ½" on all sides is included.

1.

2. Hem the front of the bonnet.

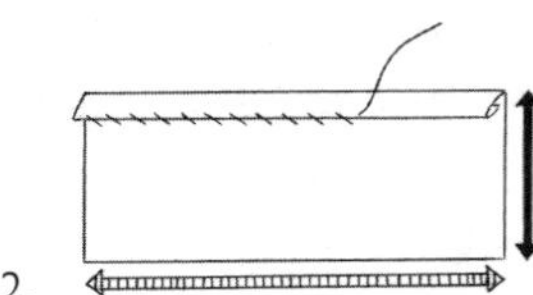
2.

3. Fold in half, right sides together, and close the back opening with a running stitch. Hem the bottom edges of the bottom.

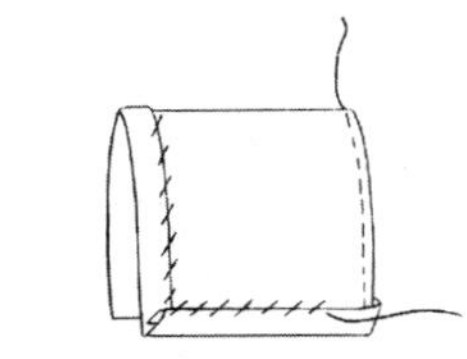
3.

Finishing Touches

4. Turn the bonnet right side out and sew on the ribbon ties.

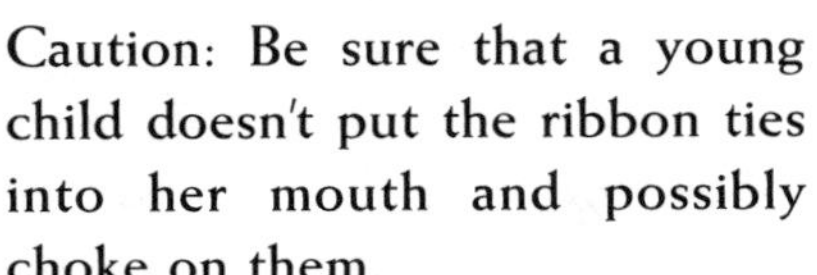
Caution: Be sure that a young child doesn't put the ribbon ties into her mouth and possibly choke on them.

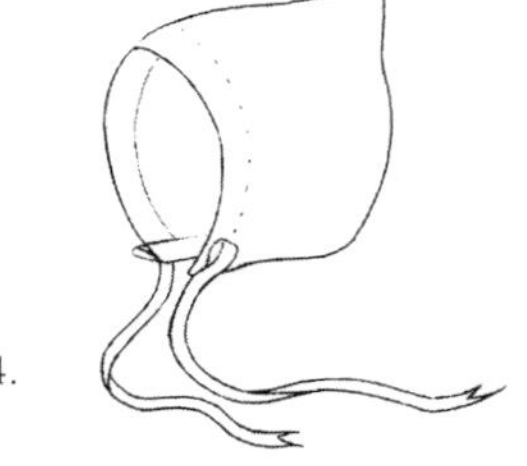
4.

Stand Up Puppets

Materials

- 6″ x 6″ cotton knit material for the head—available in many skin color shades
- medium to heavy weight wool or wool blend felt for the body—6″ x 8″
- natural colored wool batting for stuffing the head and the body
- dyed wool fleece in desired hair color plus matching thread
- additional felt, cotton or silk material for cape
- strong thread (quilting or buttonhole thread or dental floss)
- matching threads
- embroidery floss for the cape
- a flat stone (optional)

Head

1. Lay strips of natural wool batting one on top of another, as shown in the diagram. You need quite a lot of batting. Gather it up, forming a fairly firm, nice round ball for the head. The head should be about 2¼″ in diameter. Allow for the head to pack in slightly when the cotton knit is stretched over it.

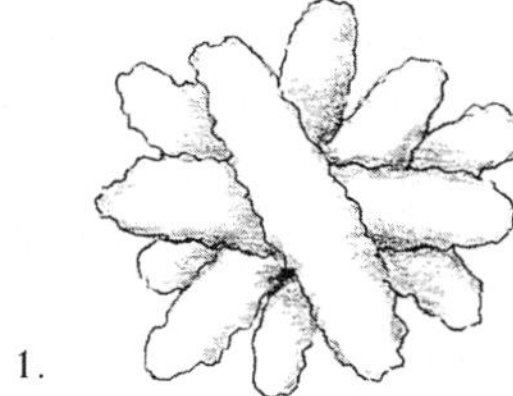

1.

The neck is very important for the finished look of the puppet. It needs to be thick enough to provide stability so the head doesn't wobble, but not too thick or it gives the impression of a fat neck. Tie the head off at the neck with strong thread or dental floss.

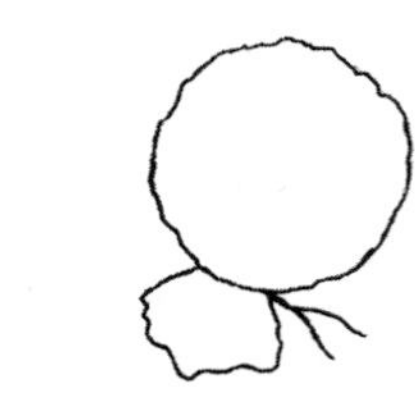

1.

2. Find the center of the square of cotton knit. Mark with pins.

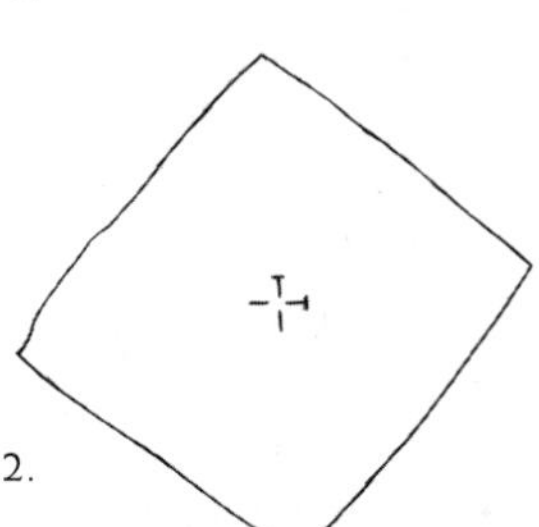

2.

3. Center head on the fabric. Stretch cotton knit fabric over the head pulling down firmly and smoothing the wrinkles in the material from one side. This smooth side will be the face of the puppet. Tie securely with strong thread or dental floss by wrapping it around the neck several times and tying tightly.

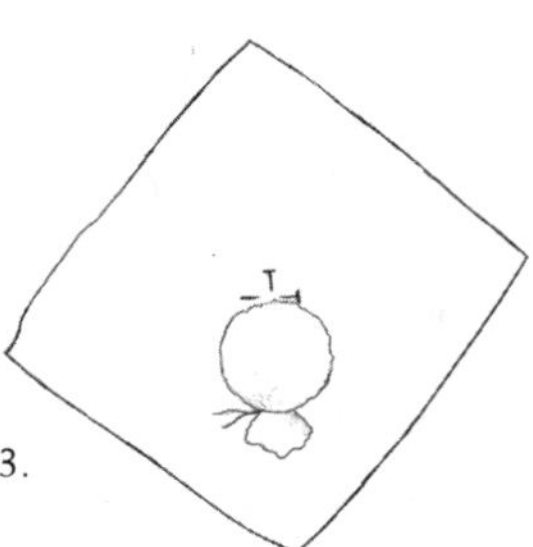

3.

Body

4. With right sides facing each other, sew a ¼″ seam up the back of the felt. Turn the felt right side out.

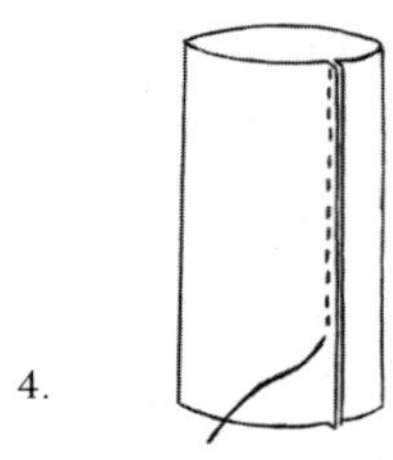

4.

5. Sew a running stitch along the neck edge using double thread, sewing close to the neck edge. Insert the head taking care to center it on the body with the face facing towards the front and the back of the head facing the seam.

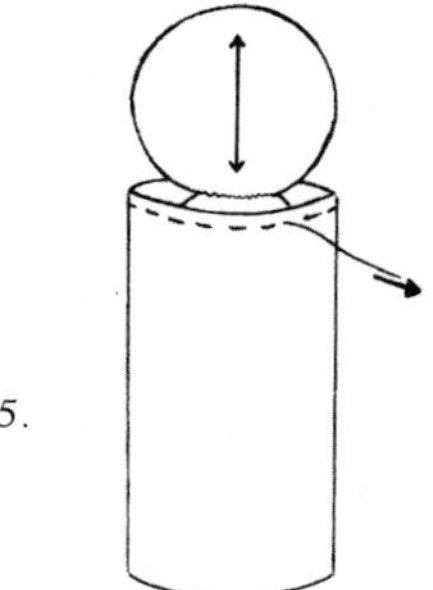
5.

Pull the thread to gather tightly around the neck. Evenly distribute the gathers and knot the thread.

Sew all around the neck edge with invisible stitches to attach the head to the body. You may need to do this several times so that the head doesn't wobble.

Finishing Touches

6. Sew on colored fleece for the hair. If your stitches show when you are finished, fluff the hair a bit to help hide them. You can also use wool yarn for hair.

6.

Felt, cotton or silk material can be used to make a cape. It should be a little shorter than the body, but similar in width. A running stitch of embroidery floss is sewn along the top of the cape for the tie.

You have two choices for finishing the bottom of the puppet.

For Hemmed Bottom

This hem provides added weight and helps the puppet stand better. Turn under ½″ for a hem and sew with the blind stitch. Stuff the puppet lightly with wool batting.

Or a Closed Bottom

You may prefer to close the bottom by ataching a circular piece of matching felt. The advantage to this method is that the stuffing doesn't come out.

Stuff the puppet body lightly with wool batting. Trace the bottom of the felt body on a piece of paper or cardboard adding ¼″ all around for seam allowance. Cut a felt circle from the pattern and stitch the circular piece onto the body adding a flat stone for weight, if you wish, just before closing entirely.

Finger Knitting

Materials:

- Bulky wool yarn (preferable to other kinds)
- Scissors
- Basket or cloth bag to hold a child's project
- Cut pieces of yarn four to five arm lengths and roll into balls or small bundles as shown.
- Use the illustrations as a guide. The arrows indicate where one holds the yarn.

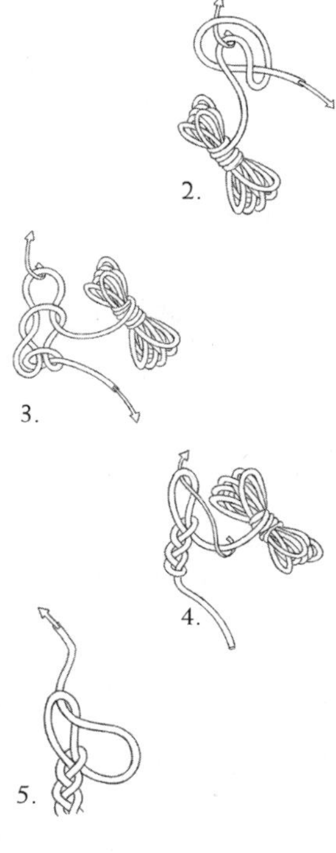

1. Cross the yarn over itself to make a loop.
2. Create a second loop by reaching through the first loop with your thumb and forefinger and grabbing the yarn. Pull it through, tightening the first loop.
3. As you continue to create new loops, hold the the finger-knitted strand firmly and near the open loop.
4. If the new loop gets too long, just pull on the long end to make it shorter.
5. To finish off the finger-knitted rope, pull the end of the yarn through the last loop and tighten.

   These ropes can be used for many items: sashes, ties for capes, fishing lines, tying packages, or even making a coiled and stitched round braided rug.

Appendix

What is Waldorf Education?

Waldorf education is a worldwide system of education for preschool through grade 12 developed from the indications of Rudolf Steiner. Steiner, an Austrian scientist, educator and writer, turned his attention to education after the First World War at the request of Emil Molt, who helped him found a school for the children of the workers at the Waldorf-Astoria cigarette factory in Stuttgart in 1919. The impulse for "Waldorf education" as it came to be called, spread throughout Europe, with the first school in America being founded in New York City in 1928.

Steiner was a pioneer in the area of developmentally based, age-appropriate learning, and many of his indications were later born out by the work of Gesell, Piaget and others. In addition, he sought to develop a balanced education for the "whole child," one which would engage the child's feeling and willing, as well as thinking, and would leave his or her spiritual nature acknowledged, but free. From preschool through high school, the goal of Waldorf education is the same, but the means differ according to the changing inner development of the child.

Waldorf Schools were closed by the Nazis during World War II, but soon reopened and have spread in the last two decades to such troubled areas as South Africa, Middle East, Eastern Europe, and the former Soviet block countries. Currently, there are more than 750 Waldorf/Steiner Schools in 46 countries.

Early Childhood Education

During the early childhood years, the child is surrounded by a home-like environment which encourages imaginative free play and artistic activity. Steiner recognized that the young child learns primarily through example and imitation, with an emphasis on the importance of movement, rhythm, fairy tales and oral language. Steiner felt that it is not healthy for children to concentrate on cognitive skills such as reading, writing, and math until the body has reached a certain level of maturity, freeing the forces of growth for cognitive work. This change is signified by many signs, including the eruption of the adult teeth and the child's ability to reach over it's head and touch the opposite ear. Children are carefully evaluated for readiness for first grade, and most schools request that children turn six *before* school starts.

Many schools have mixed-age kindergartens, with children from 3-6 years old in the same room. Typical daily activities in the preschool/kindergarten include free play, movement games, story circle, and a craft or artistic activity (water color painting, beeswax modeling, coloring with beeswax crayons, baking, and so forth). Puppet plays, nature walks and celebrating the festivals are frequent events throughout the year.

The Elementary Grades

In the elementary school (grades 1-8), all of the subjects are presented in a lively and pictorial way, because Steiner found the elementary-school child learns best when information is artistically and imaginatively presented. The same teacher stays with the same children from first through eighth grade, teaching the "morning lesson" subjects, which include language arts, mathematics, history and the sciences. This lesson is taught during the first two hours of the morning in blocks of three to six weeks per topic. Students create their own "lesson books" as artistic records of their learning, rather than using textbooks or worksheets. During the rest of the day, special subject teachers fill out the curriculum with two foreign languages, orchestra, singing, arts, crafts, gardening, eurythmy (a movement art developed by Rudolf Steiner) and physical education.

The Waldorf High School

The adolescent's emerging powers of analytical thinking are met and developed in the Waldorf high school, where subjects are taught by specialists in their fields. The role of the teacher is seen as helping the students to develop their own thinking powers. A key to this process is presenting students with an immediate experience of phenomena, such as hands-on experiments or primary sources in literature and history—instead of predigested work from textbooks or anthologies. The rapidly changing psychological nature of the adolescent is addressed through each year's studies being tailored to the central "questions" that live in the hearts of the students of that grade.

—Rahima Baldwin-Dancy, former Waldorf Early Childhood Teacher
and Author of *You Are Your Child's First Teacher*

Waldorf Education Resources

Association of Waldorf Schools of North America
AWSNA
337 Oak Grove St
Minneapolis, MN 55403
Phone: 612-870-8310
Fax: 612-870-8316
Email: awsna@awsna.org
www.waldorfeducation.org

Waldorf Early Childhood Association of North America
WECAN
285 Hungry Hollow Road
Chestnut Ridge, NY 10977
Phone: 914-352-1690
Fax: 914-352-1695
Email: info@waldorfearlychildhood.org
www.waldorfearlychildhood.org

Steiner Schools Fellowship
Kidbrooke Park, Forest Row
Sussex, RH18 5JB UK
Phone: + 44 1342 822 115
Fax: + 44 1342 826 004
www.steinerwaldorf.org.uk

Pedagogical Section at the Goetheanum
P.O. Box, CH-4143
Dornach (Switzerland)

Bob & Nancy's Services/The Waldorfshop Network/WaldorfWorld
304 Tasman Place
Philomath, OR 97370
Phone: 541-929-2359
Email: writeus@bobnancy.com
www.waldorfbooks.com or www.bobnancy.com or
www.waldorfshop.net or www.waldorfworld.net

What is Anthroposophy?

Ronald E. Koetzsch in his book, *The Parents' Guide to Alternatives in Education* introduces the reader to Rudolf Steiner and Anthroposophy:

> Steiner was an important figure in European cultural life. For many years he was head of the Theosophical Society in Germany, and in 1913 he founded a spiritual and cultural movement called Anthroposophy — 'knowlege of the true nature of the human being.' Lecturing and writing on such topics as philosophy, religion, psychology, art, history, economics, and politics, Steiner had attracted a large, sophisticated, and international following. He urged that modern humanity awaken to the reality of the spirit, both in the individual human being and in the universe as a whole, and that individual and social life be based on this reality."[1]

Steiner himself described Anthroposophy as "awareness of one's humanity." Nowhere is the need for such an awareness greater than in relation to our fellow human beings, and to the life and work we share with them. It is this awareness that is at the heart of the practical work — education, biodynamic farming, the arts, etc. — developed by Steiner.

Anthroposophy embraces a spiritual view of the human being and the cosmos, but its emphasis is on knowing, not faith. It is a path in which the human heart and hand, and especially our capacity for thinking, are essential. It leads, in Steiner's words, "from the spirit in the human being to the spirit in the universe." Humanity (*anthropos*) has the inherent wisdom (*sophia*) to transform both itself and the world.

For many people Anthroposophy's vision of human potential is a source of hope and renewal.[2]

---

1 Ronald E. Koetzsch, *The Parents' Guide to Alternatives in Education*, (Boston: Shambala Publications, 1997), 216.

2 Anthroposophical Society in America. *Towards a More Human Future, Anthroposophy at Work*, 1993.

Anthroposophical Resources

Anthroposophical Society in America
1923 Geddes Avenue
Ann Arbor, MI 48104-1797
Phone: 734-662-9355
Fax: 734-662-1727
Email: information@anthroposophy.org
www.anthroposophy.org

Bob & Nancy's Services
The WaldorfShop Network/WaldorfWorld
304 Tasman Place,
Philomath, OR 97370
Phone: 541-929-2359
Email: writeus@bobnancy.com
www.waldorfbooks.com or www.bobnancy.com
www.waldorfshop.net or www.waldorfworld.net

For other national societies, contact:
General Anthroposophical Society
P. O. Box, CH-4143 Dornach 1, Switzerland
Phone: +41 61 706 42 42
Fax: +41 61 706 43 14
Email: sekretariat@goetheanum.ch

Recommendations for Further Reading

Dollmaking, Toys and Crafts

Berger, Petra: *Feltcraft: Making Dolls, Gifts and Toys*

Detailed instructions, patterns and bright colorful photographs help the beginner and advanced crafter with making small dolls, finger and glove puppets, animals, wristbands, little gifts and even wall tapestries.

Cooper, Stephanie; Marye Rowling & Christine Fynes-Clinton: *The Children's Year*

A treasury of over 100 crafts to make with and for children, including clothing, soft items, wooden and moving toys, with some festival and seasonal themes.

Jaffke, Freya: *Toymaking with Children*

Out of her long experience as a kindergarten teacher, the author includes plans for imaginative and high quality toys such as wooden boats, log trains, doll's furniture, rag dolls, puppets, and soft animals.

Jaffke, Freya: *Making Soft Toys*

Tells how to make simple children's toys (puppets, dolls, and special surprises) with very little cost and using only natural materials.

Kraul, Walter: *Earth, Water, Fire, and Air*

Shows how to make a waterwheel, paddle-steamer, propeller plane, parachute, windmill, spinning tops, a little hot-air carousel, a hot-air balloon, and lots more. Some suggestions are simple enough for six-year olds, others challenging enough for a skillful twelve-year old.

Neuschutz, Karin: *The Doll Book: Soft Dolls and Creative Free Play*

This charming book not only gives instructions on making soft cloth dolls, but also discusses how children play at different ages.

Ping, Janene: *Felting Activity From the Kindergarten*

Produced by the Hawthorne Valley Waldorf School, this booklet gives directions for making gnome's beards and Easter eggs.

Reinckens, Sunnhild: *Making Dolls*

Instructions for seventeen dolls, including finger puppets, baby dolls, gnomes and many more.

Smith, Susan: *Echoes of a Dream; Creative Beginnings for Parent and Child*
For pre-school and kindergarten. Contents include: a child's garden, playthings and crafts, and the language of watercolors and crayons.

Wernhard, Hannelore: *The Knitted Farmyard; Knitted Gnomes and Fairies; Knit an Enchanted Castle*

Games

Brooking-Payne, Kim: *Games Children Play*
Games, both fun and therapeutic for ages three and up, that enhance teamwork, coordination, and spatial awareness. Also includes a description of why each game is helpful and needed at a particular age based on the author's extensive experience.

Büchen, Hajo; *Button, Button, Who's Got the Button: 101 Button Games*

Cole, Joanna: *Anna Banana: 101 Jump-Rope Rhymes*
Rhymes to help children keep rhythm while jumping rope

Mercury Press: *Finger Plays*
Forty-six kindergarten finger plays

van Haren, Wil & Rudolf Kischnick: *Child's Play 1 & 2: Games for Life for Children*
Ranging from simple guessing games, games using boards or table-tops, to games of imagination, wit and creativity.

von Heider, Molly: *Looking Forward*
A range of games, rhymes, songs and exercises for children aged three to eleven years. The second part of the book presents a practical and imaginative approach to teaching gardening that covers basic principles as well as projects.

Nature and Gardening

Brennan, Georgeanne & Ethel: *The Children's Kitchen Garden: A Book of Gardening, Cooking, and Learning*
Inspired by the French tradition of teaching children to appreciate fresh and healthy foods, this guide is enlivened by full color illustrations, photographs, and delightful quotes.

Cornell, Joseph: *Sharing Nature with Children*
Includes games and activities to inspire love for the natural world.

Sharing the Joy of Nature
More games and activities.

Dannenmaier, Molly: *A Child's Garden: Enchanted Outdoor Spaces for Children and Parents*
An outstanding book for parents, teachers, gardeners, and landscape designers — anyone who wants to create special places for children to play. Spectacular color photos.

Harrer, Dorothy: *Nature Ways: In Story and Verse*
Delightfully illustrated stories to be read aloud (kindergarten). Includes "The Prince of the Butterflies", "The Princes of the Golden Stairs", "The Boy and the Tree " and others.

Horsefall, Jaqueline: *Play Lightly on the Earth: Nature Activities for Children 3 to 9 Years Old*
Packed with activities that emphasize creative thinking, problem solving, and skill development cloaked in the guise of play.

Lovejoy, Sharon: *Hollyhock Days: Garden Adventures for the Young at Heart*
How children and adults can discover the magic in gardening together.

Sunflower Houses: Garden Discoveries for Children of All Ages

Leeuwen, M.V. and J. Moeskops: *The Nature Corner*
Colorful seasonal nature tables created with simple materials and basic knitting and crocheting skills.

Petrash, Carol: *Earthways, Simple Environmental Activities for Young Children*
Filled with hands-on nature crafts and seasonal activities to enhance environmental awareness carefully described and beautifully illustrated.

Songs, Verses, Prayers and Celebrations

Barz, Brigitte: *Festivals with Children*
Offers a description of the nature and character of each Christian

festival, its symbols and customs, and gives practical suggestions for celebrating these festivals in the family.

Berger, Thomas: *The Christmas Craft Book, The Easter Craft Book, The Harvest Craft Book,*

This series of books offers a wealth of ideas for seasonal decorations with easy to follow directions and accompanying bright colorful pictures. Teachers and parents will refer to these for years.

Burton, Michael: *In the Light of a Child: Fifty-two Verses for Children and the Child in Every Human Being*

These verses, following the course of the year, were inspired by Rudolf Steiner's Calendar of the Soul and are arranged for both hemispheres.

Capel, Evelyn Francis: *Celebrating Festivals Around the World*

Should the festivals be tied to nature's cycle or the Christian year? The author delves into what lies behind the rhythms of the natural year, describing the part played by archangels and elementals.

Carey, Diana and Judy Large: *Festivals, Family and Food*

A resource book for exploring the festivals. Grouped into the four seasons with sections on birthdays, teatimes, rainy days, etc. Over 650 songs, games for fun, food to make, stories, poems and things to do.

Cooper, Stephanie, Christine Fynes-Clinton and Mary Rowling: *The Children's Year*

Here is a book that takes us through the seasons with appropriate toys and gifts to create. Includes full, clear instructions and illustrations.

Carter, Robin: *The Tao and Mother Goose: Myth and Meaning in Nursery Rhymes*

This art instructor's illustrated book is both enjoyable and informative. Rhymes of Mother Goose, he suggests, frequently are spiritual parables. Consequently, a simple word, phrase, or idea in this meditative picture book might kindle a spark deep within the reader.

Druitt, Ann and Christine Fynes-Clinton and Marije Rowling: *All Year Round*

Designed to help families create their own traditions using this book as a springboard. Brimming with stories, poems, activities, things to make and songs.

Eliot, Jane Winslow: *Let's Talk Let's Play: Helping Children Learn How to Learn from Life*

Practical guide for parents, includes lessons, songs, games, poems and celebrations.

Fitzjohn, Sue and Minda Weston and Judy Large: *Festivals Together: A Guide to Multi-Cultural Celebrations*

This resource guide seeks to enrich and widen our celebration experiences and to reflect the 'global village' nature of modern society.

Foster, Nancy: *Dancing as We Sing: Seasonal Circle Plays & Traditional Singing Games*

An experienced Waldorf early childhood teacher shares her collection.

Green Marian: *A Calendar of Festivals: Traditional Celebrations, Songs, Seasonal Recipes & Things to Make*

From holy days to holidays, high days to hey days, every month is a festival. This book explores the fascinating details of seasonal customs — what they are, what they represent, their original meaning, where they are continued and their relevance to us today.

Jaffke, Christophe and Magda Maier: *Early One Morning: Folk Songs, Rounds, Ballads, Shanties, Spirituals and Plantations Songs, and Madrigals.*

A book which has a diverse selection of music for parents, teachers and children. Another important resource.

Jones, Betty: *A Child's Seasonal Treasury*

This beautiful collection of poems, songs, finger games, crafts, and recipes presents hundreds of ways to incorporate the seasons in children's play, gleaned from the author's many years as a Waldorf teacher.

Middleton, Julie Forest: *Songs for Earthlings: A Green Spirituality Songbook*

A songbook of Earth songs, God/Goddess songs, songs for the cycles of life, songs of love for the inhabitants of this planet. Text describes how to live carefully and gently so that life on Earth might continue.

Metropolitan Museum of Art: *Go In and Out the Window: An Illustrated Songbook for Young People*

Sixty-one classic childhood songs, includes work songs, play songs, nursery songs, lullabies, and ballads

Nelson, Gudrud Mueller: *To Dance With God: Family Ritual and Community Celebration*

Makes relevant for the modern reader the importance of ritual for connecting us to the meaning and flow of life.

Powers, Mala: *Follow the Year: A Family Celebration of Christian Holidays*

Helps today's family, whatever the denomination, to understand and follow the rhythm of the Christian festivals through the course of the entire year. Out of print, but worth searching for.

Scott, Anne: *The Laughing Baby: Remembering Nursery Rhymes and Reasons*

The author explains how this enchanting form of play - the use of rhythmic sounds and sensations — strengthens the bonds between adult and child and is integral to the child's development and well-being.

Society of Brothers: *Sing Through the Day: Ninety Songs for Younger Children*

Songs for getting up in the morning, going to bed, playing, dancing, birthdays, thanksgiving, Easter, Christmas, animals, and even songs about the rain are in this international collection.

Sing Through the Seasons: Ninety-nine Songs for Children

Some songs were written by the Society of Brothers while others appear for the first time in English, translated from the German, along with old favorites and international songs to inspire all ages.

Steiner, Rudolf: *Prayers for Parents and Children*

Verses for every occasion. Based on Rudolf Steiner's philosophy of the larger cosmic relationships before birth, during life, and after death. Includes his lecture on the subject.

Thomas, Anne & Peter: *The Children's Party Book: For Birthdays and Other Occasions*

Full of ideas for games and craft activities, puppet shows, parties with a theme, decorations, invitations, etc.

Waldorf Association of Early Childhood in North America (WECAN): *Let Us Form a Ring*

Songs, verses and stories for kindergarten circle-time categorized according to the season, birthdays and time of day.

Waskow, Arthur: *Seasons of Our Joy: A Modern Guide to the Jewish Holidays*

Origins, practices, new approaches, recipes and songs are included in this guide leading the reader on a spiritual journey through the year.

Storytelling, Plays, and Puppet Shows

Mellon, Nancy: *The Art of Storytelling*

This ancient art is an antidote to today's world of electronic entertainment. Learn how to create a magical atmosphere for the telling of tales, discover the subtle ingredients of storytelling and the symbolism which represent archetypal forces in our world.

Wilkinson, Roy: *Plays for Puppets*

Based on well known fairy tales for kindergarten age. Adaptable for silk marionettes.

Zahlingen, Bronja: *A Lifetime of Joy* (formerly *Plays for Puppets and Marionettes*)

A collection of fairy tales adapted for use as kindergarten puppet plays, with accompanying verses and songs. Instructions for making marionettes included.

Parenting

Baldwin-Dancy, Rahima: *You Are Your Child's First Teacher*

A rich resource for parents of young children, written by a former Waldorf early education teacher. Contains sections on receiving and caring for the newborn, helping your toddler's development, and parenting issues of the first three years.

Britz-Crecelius, Heidi: *Children at Play: Using Waldorf Principles to Foster Childhood Development*

The author, a mother and proponent of Waldorf education, recommends specific games, toys and art supplies that aid in the unfoldment of imagination.

Coplen, Dotty: *Parenting: A Path Through Childhood*

Combining her experience as a mother and grandmother with her studies in psychology and social work the author presents her insights into the nature and needs of children.

Parenting for a Healthy Future

Practical and spiritual perspective into the challenge of parenting.

Darian, Shea: *Seven Times the Sun:Guiding your Child Through the Rhythms of the Day*

Practical and playful. The author shows how to bring joy to such daily events as mealtimes, bedtimes, chores, and naps.

Davy, Gudrun and Bons Voors: *Lifeways: Working with Family Questions*

A collection of essays for the '90s on the meaning of "home" and the tension between personal fulfillment and family life.

More Lifeways: Finding Support and Inspiration in Family Life, edited by Patti Smith & Signe E. Schaefer

Twenty-seven articles on themes such as: listening, inner development, money, sex and power, spirituality, single parenting, fathering, death and dying in the family, adoption.

Elium, Don & Jeanne: *Raising a Family: Living on Planet Parenthood*

This book is about how to create a care oriented environment where families are a group arriving together at the same destination rather than individuals pulling in separate directions.

Raising a Son: Parents and the Making of a Healthy Man

Among the first to address the challenges of raising boys to become healthy, assertive, and loving men.

Raising A Daughter: Parents and the Awakening of a Healthy Woman

Helps parents unravel the conflicting messages girls receive from our culture and address the ever changing social attitudes.

Elkind, David: *Growing Up Too Fast Too Soon*
Gives parents and teachers insight and hope for encouraging healthy development while protecting the joy and freedom of childhood.

The Hurried Child: Growing Up Too Fast Too Soon
Children today are being pushed both cognitively and emotionally before they are developmentally ready, mimmicking adult sophistication while secretely yearning for innocense.

The Ties That Stress: The New Family Imbalance
Sums up the changes in the American family in the last few decades and the cost to children.

Fenner, Pamela and Karen Rivers: *Waldorf Student Reading List*, revised 3rd edition, 1995
Comprehensive reading list to help parents, teachers, librarians, and home schools select quality books for children.

Glöckler, Michaela and Wolfgang Goebel: *A Guide to Child Health*
This is a medical and educational handbook written out of many years' experience in the consulting rooms at the large anthroposophical hospital in Herdecke, W. Germany.

Haller, Ingeborg: *How Children Play*
Imaginative play is a vital element in the growth of the preschool child. A child's freedom to play lies at the root of a happy and well-balanced attitude to work and responsibilities in later life.

Healy MD, Jane: *Endangered Minds: Why Children Don't Think and What We Can Do About It*
This book explores the relationship between language, learning, and brain development. The author explains how present-day lifestyles sabotage language acquisition and thinking.

Jones, Noraugh: *In Search of Home: Women Working, Caring ,Sharing*
The author listens to women living through serial relationships, single parenting, lesbian couples, divorced and separated individuals, women left alone in old age, travellers and creative solitaries. Each creates her own version of "home," which may bear little resemblance

to tradition, but reflect a path travelled toward emotional and moral maturity.

Kane, Franklin: *Parents as People*
A veteran Waldorf teacher describes the life of the young growing child and the importance of rhythm. His interpretation of Waldorf education and Steiner's philosophy is presented in an easy-to-read style with little jargon.

Lievegoed, Bernard: *Phases of Childhood: Growing in Body, Soul and Spirit*
Explores the cycles of child development in the light of the ideas of Rudolf Steiner. One of the most read and re-read books for many Waldorf parents and teachers.

Pearce, Joseph Chilton: *Evolution's End: Claiming the Potential of our Intelligence*
Employs both the results of academic research and personal experience to develop his thesis on the evolution of human intelligence. He offers some far-reaching insights into the challenges and obstacles to human development created by our culture.

The Magical Child
Discusses the phases every child goes through as he matures, emphasizing that there is a time for everything. This means not "abandoning" the child in the crib, not pushing the preschooler to learn to read, limiting television viewing and encouraging fantasy and play.

The Magical Child Matures
May be out of print, but worth looking for in a library.

Querido, Rene: *The Wonder of Childhood*
Describes the first three years in the life of the child.

Salter, Joan: *The Incarnating Child*
A specialist in maternal and child care, Salter examines pregnancy, birth, and childhood on up to adolescence, addressing both physical and spiritual development, health, environment, and learning.

Mothering with Soul: Raising Children as Special Work
Raising children, a career of the heart, is seen as spiritual activity, not

merely a practical job; includes sections on expecting, birthing, breastfeeding, rhythms of the day, evolution of consciousness, work outside the family, childcare, grandmothers, and more.

Sanders, Barry: *A Is for Ox: The Collapse of Literacy and the Rise of Violence in an Electronic Age*

The author challenges the reader to redefine what literacy is, how it evolves from oral culture, and why it is essential. A program for nurturing literacy is presented.

Schmidt-Brabant, Manfred: *The Spiritual Tasks of the Homemaker*

How to use spiritual knowledge to bring strength and insight to the modern homemaker.

Solter, Ph.D., Aletha J.: *The Aware Baby*

The author questions most of the traditional beliefs about childrearing and describes a new theory that is useful and practical as well as far-reaching in its implications.

Helping Young Children Flourish

The author presents her insights into young children's emotions, and describes effective alternatives to both punishments and rewards.

Thomson, John general editor: *Natural Childhood: The First Practical and Holistic Guide for Parents of the Developing Child.*

The ideas of enlightened thinkers such as Rudolf Steiner, John Holt, and Carl Rogers provide new insights into the internal development of the child. Explores a wealth of new ideas as well as the more traditional aspects of relationships, education, health, creativity, and play.

von Heydebrand, Caroline: *Childhood: A Study of the Growing Child*

This book weaves together various approaches to child development, physiology, and the temperaments as well as insights from Rudolf Steiner, of whom she was a direct student.

zur Linden, Wilhelm: *A Child is Born: Pregnancy, Birth, First Childhood*

Indications for proper care, nutrition and upbringing from a lifetime's experience as a pediatrician and general practitioner with the understanding of the three-fold nature of the human being (body, soul spirit).

Television and Technology

Armstrong, Alison & Charles Casement: *The Child and the Machine: Why Computers May Put Our Child's Education at Risk*
Draws on scientific and medical studies, groundbreaking in the depth and rigor of its research, credible in its conclusions.

Buzzell, Keith: *The Children Of Cyclops: The Influence of Television Vewing On the Developing Human Brain*
Does the experience of watching television negatively affect the cognitive development of a growing child? New research.

Healy, Jane: *Failure to Connect: How Computers Affect Our Children's Minds — for Better or Worse*
Important addition to the debate about how much of a good thing it is to mix computers and children.

Large, Martin: *Who's Bringing Them Up? How to Break the T.V. Habit*
Effects of television on children and families and suggestions for cutting down viewing.

Winn, Marie: *The Plug-In Drug: Television, Children and the Family*
Examines the effects of passive watching of T.V., video games, and computers on the developing child.

Waldorf Education

There are many excellent books for those interested in knowing more about Waldorf education. If these books by Rudolf Steiner and others are not available in a local library or bookstore, they can be ordered from the Waldorf, Anthroposophical, and Publisher Resources listed.

Almon, Joan: *An Overview of the Waldorf Kindergarten*
Articles from the Waldorf Kindergarten Newsletter 1981-1992, Volume I, a practical guide.

Appendix

Almon, Joan: *A Deeper Understanding of the Waldorf Kindergarten*
Articles from the Waldorf Kindergarten Newsletter 1981-1992, Volume II, about the spiritual background of the young child's development.

Edmunds, Francis: *Rudolf Steiner Education*
A most respected figure in English speaking Waldorf schools authoritatively answers the question, 'What is a Waldorf school?'

Fenner, Pamela & Karen Rivers: *Waldorf Education, A Family Guide*
A collection of articles that guides one through the world of Waldorf education. Addresses the questions and concerns of parents as well as creates clear pictures for understanding. Highly recommended for new Waldorf parents.

Finser, Torin: *School as a Journey: The Eight-Year Odyssey of a Waldorf Teacher and His Class*
An engrossing, personal narrative about a Waldorf teacher and his class.

Grunelius, Elisabeth: *Early Childhood Education*
This pioneer work describes the organization and purposes of the Waldorf kindergarten, including the layout of a kindergarten, indoor and outdoor equipment, and the rhythms of the day.

Harwood, A. C.: *The Recovery of Man in Childhood: A Study of the Educational Work of Rudolf Steiner*
A lucid presentation of the Waldorf approach from preschool through 12th grade. Highly recommended for in-depth description of theoretical and practical aspects of this education.

Harwood, A. C.: *The Way of a Child*
One of the most popular introductions to child development and Waldorf education.

Heckman, Helen: *Nøkken: A Garden for Children*
Describes a Danish approach to Waldorf-based childcare.

Howard, Alan: *You Wanted to Know.... What a Waldorf School is.... and What It is Not*
Written by a leading Waldorf educator, this small book is designed in

a question-and-answer format. It answers basic questions concerning the history of Waldorf education, the learning experience, and school/community relationships.

Koetzsch, Ronald E.: *The Parent's Guide to Alternatives in Education*
The first in-depth guide to the full range of choices in alternative schooling, with all the information you need to decide what kind of education is right for your child.

Pusch, Ruth, editor: *Waldorf Schools, Volume I and II*
A collection of articles on every aspect of Waldorf education. These were published over almost 40 years of Education as an Art, the bulletin from the Rudolf Steiner School of New York City. Volume I, early childhood; Volume II, upper grades.

Querido, René M.: *Creativity in Education: The Waldorf Approach*
Describes a Waldorf educational approach that has as its goal the balanced development of the whole child.

Steiner, Rudolf: *An Introduction to Waldorf Education, The Kingdom of Childhood, The Child's Changing Consciousness,* and many others.
Contact Rudolf Steiner College Press and Bookstore for catalogue.

Steiner, Rudolf: *Foundations of Waldorf Education Series*
New series which will contain all of Rudolf Steiner's lectures and writings on Waldorf Education in English. Contact Anthroposophical Press for catalogue.

von Heydebrand, Caroline: *Childhood*
This is the classic work on the Waldorf kindergarten. Heydebrand worked with Rudolf Steiner at the first Waldorf School, and her book contains a wealth of insights about working with preschoolers.

Waldorf Early Childhood Association of North America (WECAN): *The Waldorf Kindergarten Newsletter Spring 1998*
This collection of articles written by kindergarten experts, also includes activities, songs and stories. Health issues, international work and research are some of the features.

Wilkinson, Roy: *Commonsense Schooling* and *Renewing Education*
A practical introduction to Rudolf Steiner's educational thought and methodology. It examines such topics as the purpose of education, the nature of the child, and the structure and organization of the school.

Videos

Taking a Risk in Education: Waldorf Inspired Public Schools: 48 min.
This presentation showcases how Waldorf curriculum is being integrated into public schools across the U.S. A first-hand look at the teachers, administrators, and students working and learning within these programs.

The Waldorf Promise: 53 min.
Eight public school teachers who use Waldorf education in their classrooms share their classroom experiences as well as personal ones.

Urban Waldorf: A Day in the Life of a Milwaukee Public School: 20 min.
A documentary on how the Waldorf curriculum is being utilized to enliven and improve public education in the U.S.

Waldorf Education: A Vision of Wholeness: 16 min.
An active view of curriculum in several Waldorf schools with teachers, students, and parents.

Anthroposophy

Readers are encouraged to send for catalogues from Anthroposophic Press, Mercury Press, and Rudolf Steiner College Press for an extensive list of works in English by Rudolf Steiner as well as biographies. The following are just a few selections:

Barnes, Henry: *A Life for the Spirit: Rudolf Steiner in the Crosscurrents of Our Time*
Recounts the dynamic life of Rudolf Steiner, an active leader whose entire being was given in service to humanity and to the spirit and places him in the crosscurrents of history.

Easton, Stewart: *The Way of Anthroposophy —Answers to Modern Questions*
This small book serves as an introduction to Anthroposophy by one of the most noted interpreters of Rudolf Steiner.

Easton, Stewart: *Man and World in the Light of Anthroposophy*

Outlines the teachings of the many areas in which Steiner made his contributions, providing the reader with an appreciation of the enormous wealth of richness of what Rudolf Steiner gave to mankind.

McDermott, Robert, editor: *The Essential Steiner*

An accessible introduction to Rudolf Steiner's thought and work. With introductory essays by McDermott and 17 selections from Steiner's books and lectures, this book is considered by many students of Anthroposophy to be indispensable.

Sedden, Richard, editor: *Understanding the Human Being*

Carefully selected anthology of works by Rudolf Steiner gives a panoramic view of his fundamental ideas in a wide range of topics.

Soesman, Albert: *The Twelve Senses*

Presents a lively way of experiencing and understanding the human senses in light of the work of Steiner. This imaginative approach makes this an accessible study guide for teachers, doctors, therapists, counselors, psychologists, and scientists.

Steiner, Rudolf: *The Course of My Life* (Steiner's autobiography)

The following titles are considered the "basic books" of Anthroposophy, containing the essential nature of Rudolf Steiner's teachings:

How to Know Higher Worlds, a Modern Path of Initiation (book and audio versions)

Intuitive Thinking as a Spiritual Path, A Philosophy of Freedom (formerly titled *The Philosophy of Freedom* or *The Philosophy of Spiritual Activity*)

An Outline of Esoteric Science (formerly titled: *An Outline of Occult Science*)

Theosophy, An Introduction to the Spiritual Processes in Human Life and in the Cosmos

Christianity as Mystical Fact

Publisher Resources

AWSNA Publications
Renewal Production and Sales
3911 Bannister Road
Fair Oaks, CA 95628
Phone: 916-961-0927
Fax: 916-961-0715
Email: publications@awsna.org
www.waldorfeducation.org

Mercury Press
241 Hungry Hollow Road
Chestnut Ridge, NY 10977
Phone: 914-425-9357
Fax: 914-425-2107

Michaelmas Press
P.O. Box 702
Amesbury, MA 01913-0016
Phone: 978-388-7066
Fax: 978-388-6031
Email: info@michaelmaspress.com
www.michaelmaspress.com

Rudolf Steiner College Press
9200 Fair Oaks Blvd
Fair Oaks, CA 95628
Phone: 916-961-8729
Fax: 916-961-3032
Email: orders@steinercollege.edu
www.steinercollege.edu

Steiner Schools Fellowship
Publications
Kidbrooke Park, Forest Row
Sussex, RH18 5JB UK
Phone: + 44 1342 822 115
Fax: + 44 1342 826 004
www.steinerwaldorf.org.uk

SteinerBooks
Anthroposophic Press
PO Box 960
Herndon, VA 20172-0960
Phone: (703) 661-1594
Toll free in US: 1-800-856-8664
Fax: (703) 661-1501
Toll-free fax in US: 1-800-277-7947
Email: service@steinerbooks.org
www.steinerbooks.org

Sources of Supplies

The following is a short selection of suppliers of particular interest to early childhood parents and teachers. These vendors may offer materials for making items as well as finished products. Lists of suppliers are also available through the Waldorf Early Childhood Association (WECAN) and other Waldorf Education resources.

Multiple items: Dolls, Crafts, Toys, etc.

A Child's Dream Come True
1223-D Michigan Street
Sandpoint, Idaho 83864
Toll-free in US: 1-800-359-2906
Email: info@achildsdream.com
www.achildsdream.com

June Albright
Rt. 5
North Hartland, VT 05052
Phone: 802-221-1112

Blessings Catalog
11115 E. Shady Lane
Tucson, AZ 85749
Toll-free in US: 1-800-864-0131
Phone: 520-760-1396
Fax: 520 844-1104
Email: info@blessingscatalog.com
www.blessingscatalog.com

Creative Hands
PO Box 2217
Eugene, OR 97402
Phone: 541-343-1562
Store: 488 Willamette Street
Eugene, OR 97401

Heartwood Arts
8987A Soda Bay Road
Kelseyville, CA 95451
Toll-free phone/fax in US:
1-800-488-9469
www.heartwoodarts.com

Hedgehog Farms
8 Grand Oak Farm Road
Hadley, MA 01035
Phone/fax: 413-586-5267
www.hedgehogfarms.com

Magic Cabin
PO Box 1049
Madison, VA 22727-1049
Toll-free in US: 1-888-623-3655
Toll-free in US fax: 1-888-252-8464
www.magiccabin.com

Mercurius USA
4321 Anthony Court, Unit 5
Rocklin, CA 95677
Phone: 916-652-9696
Fax: 916-652-5221
Email: info@mercurius-usa.com

Nova Natural Toys and Crafts
140 Webster Road
Shelburne, VT 05482
Toll-free in US: 1-877-668-2111
Fax: 802-304-9167
Email: info@novanatural.com
www.novanatural.com

Paper, Scissors, Stone
PO Box 428
Viroqua, WI 54665
Phone: 608-637-7686
Fax: 608-637-6158
www.waldorfsupplies.com

Rudolf Steiner College Bookstore
9200 Fair Oaks Boulevard
Fair Oaks, CA 95628
Phone: 916-961-8729
Fax: 916-961-3032
Email: orders@steinercollege.edu
www.steinercollege.edu

Sunbridge College Bookstore
260 Hungry Hollow Road
Chestnut Ridge, NY 10977
Phone: 845-425-0983
www.sunbridge.edu/bookstore

Weir Dolls and Crafts
2909 Parkridge Drive
Ann Arbor, MI 48103
Phone: 734-668-6992
Fax: 734-668-9320
www.weirdollsandcrafts.com

Felt

Aetna Felt Company
2401 W. Emaus Avenue
Allentown, PA 18103
Toll-free in US: 1-800-526-4451
Fax: 610-791-5791
Email: info@aetnafelt.com
www.aetnafelt.com

Silk

Ruppert, Gibbon & Spider
PO Box 425
Healdsburg, CA 95448
Toll-free in US: 1-800-442-0455
Fax: 707-433-4906
www.silkconnection.com

Sureway Trading Co.
826 Pine Ave., Suites 5 & 6
Niagara Falls, NY 14301
Phone: 416-596-1887
555 Richmond St. West, Suite 507
Toronto, ONT M5V 3B1
CANADA
Phone: 416-596-1887

Yarns

Wilde Yarns
3737 Main Street
PO Box 4662
Philadelphia, PA 19127-0662
Phone: 215-482-8800
Toll-free in US: 1-800-423-0775
Fax: 215-482-8210
www.wildeyarns.com

Kinderhof Fibers
76 Boice Road
PO Box 551
N. Egremont, MA 01252
Phone: 413-528-2485,
413-528-9297

Music

Song of the Sea
Edward and Anne Damm
47 West Street
Bar Harbor, ME 04609
Phone: 207-288-5653
Fax: 207-288-8136
Email: mail@songsea.com
www.songsea.com

Nature's Song & Rose Lyre
230 Joslen Boulevard
Hudson, NY 12513
Toll-free in US: 1-888-650-4050
Fax: 518-822-1033
Outside US: 518-822-1033
Email: susan@naturessong.com
www.naturessong.com

naturally you can sing™
Mary Thienes Schunemann
3026 South Street
East Troy, WI 53120
Toll-free in US: 1-800 640 5905
Phone: 262-642-5921
Fax: 262-642-2184
Email:
mary@naturallyyoucansing.com

Health and Cosmetics

Dr. Hauschka Skincare
59 North Street
Hatfield, MA 01038
Toll-free in US: 1-800-247-9907
www.drhauschka.com

Vidar Goods
PO Box 41
Faber, VA 22938
Phone/fax: 434-263-8895
Toll-free in US: 1-800-769-1651
Email: vidargoods@earthlink.net

Weleda, Inc.
1 Closter Road
PO Box 675
Palisades, NY 10964
Toll-free in US: 1-800-241-1030
www.usa.weleda.com

Acknowledgments

Thanks to Great Oaks School of Evanston, Illinois for sponsoring the Parent Enrichment Series which inspired *Beyond the Rainbow Bridge*. Both authors are donating their royalties to Great Oaks School.

Thank you Janet Kellman for the very gracious Foreword and to Dr. Andrea Rentea for writing about the importance of warmth—two additions which enriched our book.

Ellen Taylor gave invaluable help and support. Her scholarly background was the basis for thoroughly questioning us about our content. Many thanks to our readers: Mary Ber, Lisa Basset, Bonnie Chauncey, and Zahava Fisch. Thanks also to Dorothy Creed.

Thanks to Nancy Parsons whose editing skills and experience in Waldorf pedagogy and Anthroposophy substantiated the publication.

Cynthia Aldinger, Joan Almon, and Susan Grey Weber made helpful comments and suggestions for the fairy tale references in the book.

Claude Julien helped us move into the big world of publishing with his helpful advice in the 110 degree heat of the Sacramento, California Kolisko Conference of August, 1998.

Thanks also to Paul Carmen who gave us legal advice when we needed it. A special thankyou to Mimi Acciari, Beth Kelly, Mary Spaulding and Carol Regenhardt who were part of a focus session on "Developing the Twelve Senses" chapter.

A warm thank you to all the children and parents who were part of River Park Children's Garden over the years. They provided the depth of everyday life experience and humor that formed the backbone of our book. Some photographs in the book are of these wonderful children.

We are grateful to artist, Jean Riordan, who was an assistant and co-taught at River Park Children's Garden for four years. She created many beautiful drawings for the children's birthdays and for their memory books at kindergarten graduation. After all these years, her artwork has become family treasures. Her husband, Kevin, provided scans of the artwork for the publisher. Thank you Jean and Kevin.

Our husbands deserve a special thanks for their patience over the long haul: to Robert Patterson for his helpful advice out of his long connection with Waldorf pedagogy, as a parent, and as a board member of the Great Oaks School and to Gerry Labedz for his computer expertise, sense of humor and continued confidence in our project which served us well when our spirits lagged. Barbara enjoyed her first computer lesson with him.

Our thanks also to Pamela Fenner, who believed we had a message that parents and teachers were seeking. Her high standards and desire to produce a quality book have resulted in a beautiful publication of which we are pleased to be a part.

Lastly, we would like to acknowledge each other as co-authors:

Over the years, Barbara, you probably questioned my sanity many times and had doubts that we would ever have a real book. But you hung in there with me, even in the darkest days. Your will forces are very well developed! You have given our book such class and breathed into it such life in the sharing of your knowledge and your personal experiences. Thank you, Barbara. It has been a privilege to work with you.

Pamela, you get the star for being able to decipher my hand written notes on the manuscript with arrows pointing here and there and stars indicating where to insert new sentences. You did it all with that wonderful infectious smile of yours that kept me going. I learned so much from you and am particularly grateful to you for the creativity you brought to the book through your gift of writing. I couldn't have done it without you. Thank you, Pam.

Biographies

Barbara Patterson attended the teacher education program at the Waldorf Institute of Southern California and was an early childhood teacher at Highland Hall Waldorf School in Northridge, CA for three years. Upon moving to Chicago, she operated River Park Children's Garden out of her home for eight years.

From 1993 she was both a teacher and a member of the Board of Directors of Great Oak School in Evanston, IL. There her work included consulting, mentoring, teaching parent-child classes, as well as early childhood classes. She is formerly on the faculty of Arcturus, a Waldorf Teacher Education program in Chicago. Barbara currently teaches at the Oakland Steiner School in Rochester Hills, Michigan. She is the mother of three and a grandmother.

Pamela Bradley is a long time public relations consultant, teacher, and mother of two Chicago Waldorf School students. She was the editor of *The Home Court Advantage* by Mayer Eisenstein, M.D. and *A Midwife Reflects* by Kay Furay and numerous other publications about the safety and advisability of home birth. Pamela has a Master of Arts degree from New York University and is a published poet and repeat student of the University of Iowa Summer Writing Festival. She was co-editor of the successful annual Chicago Waldorf School calendar. Pam lives in Chicago with her husband and two daughters and is currently writing a family memoir.

Jean Riordan, cover artist and illustrator, attended the Chicago Academy of Fine Art and is an alumna of the School of the Art Institute of Chicago. Her artwork ranges from fashion to fine art. She met Barbara Patterson in 1987 and worked closely with her for the next six years, the first two years as an enthusiastic parent creating many of the things for the room and the children. Afterwards, she became an assistant and then co-taught with Barbara at River Park Children's Garden. Jean lives in Chicago with her husband and three sons.

Colophon

Manuscript: Word 5.01 on StarMax 3000/180

Cover illustration: Jean Riordan

Cover design/execution: Karen Merk
QuarkXpress, PhotoShop
Fonts: Adobe Exponto, Weiss, Americana

Interior layout: Karen Billipp, Eliot House Productions
QuarkXpress, PhotoShop
Fonts: Adobe Exponto, Weiss, Geometrica

Interior illustrations: Jean Riordan

Consultant: Dale Hushbeck

Copyeditor: Lucie Juneau Patrowicz

Printer: Thomson-Shore, Inc.

Other Publications from Michaelmas Press

- *Waldorf Education: A Family Guide*
  Edited by Pamela J. Fenner and Karen Rivers $24.95
  The #1 introduction to Waldorf Education available. This comprehensive book is a collection of articles describing Waldorf Education—curriculum, philosophy, history, celebrations and traditions. Perfect book for teachers, parents, libraries, and college classes.
  ISBN-13: 978-0-9647832-1-8

- *Books for the Journey: A Guide to the World of Reading*
  Compiled and edited by Fenner, Greer, and Wulsin $17.95
  An annotated high school reading list of nearly 1500 of the "best books ever," divided by subject: fiction, drama, poetry, biography, history, non-fiction, mythology and sacred writing. Includes a section where seniors chose the books that made a difference in their lives. A "Reader's Road Map" guides the reader through each section.
  ISBN-13: 978-0-9647832-4-9

- *Celebrating Whittier, New England's Quaker Poet and Abolitionist: America's 1907 Centennial*
  Compiled and edited by Pamela J. Fenner $19.95
  In hundreds of celebrations, Whittier was revered as a poet, editor, and politician. He served as the conscience of his nation regarding the horrific practice of slavery at a time when conscience was our nation's greatest need. 75+ photos/illustrations/documents. Published for the 2007 Bicentennial. ISBN-13: 978-0-9647832-2-5

Add $4.50 for shipping for each U.S. order. Volume discounts available.

PO Box 702
Amesbury, MA 01913-0016 USA

Phone: 978-388-7066 Email: info@michaelmaspress.com
Fax: 978-388-6031 Website: www.michaelmaspress.com